YOU LEAD YOU

SELF-LEADERSHIP INSTEAD OF SELF-SABOTAGE

TREVOR STOCKWELL

Lead Me Now Publishing

© 2024 Trevor Stockwell

Written by human intelligence, me.

All rights reserved. No part of this book may be reproduced by any mechanical, photographic, or electronic process, or in the form of an audio recording; nor may it be stored in a retrieval system, transmitted, or otherwise be copied for public or private use - other than as brief quotations in articles, posts and reviews [when referenced] - without prior written permission of the publisher.

Published by Lead Me Now Publishing

All hyperlinks and references are accurate at the time of writing but may change or cease to exist in the future. The author/publisher is not responsible or liable for any subsequent changes made or any third-party content/terms. Inclusion of these links and references does not imply endorsement of, or agreement with the entire activities, values or beliefs of an organisation or individual.

trevorstockwell.com

1st Edition 2024

E-book ISBN: 978-1-7384444-0-3

Hardcover ISBN: 978-1-7384444-1-0

Paperback ISBN: 978-1-7384444-2-7

Audiobook ISBN: 978-1-7384444-3-4

*"The art of finding true fulfilment
is in successful,
selfless,
self-leadership"*

Contents

Why this is crucial 1
Success is within reach 5
Glimpses from My Story 13
Defining Self-Leadership 21
    Selfless Self-Leadership 23
    The Selfless Superpower 25
    You are unique, on purpose! 26
    Valuing YOU 29
    Your Passion 30
    Who decides what great self-leadership is? 31
    Things to consider 32
    Exposing some self-leadership myths 33
Attributes of Successful Self-leadership 39
    Honesty 39
    Rest 41
    Self-care 43
    Emotional intelligence (EQ) 46
    Accountability 50
    Self-control 52
    Reflection 56
Outright Enemies of Successful Self-Leadership 61
    Procrastination 61
    Lack of awareness 65
    Limiting beliefs 67
    Being unteachable 72
    Distraction 74
    Selfishness 77

Stinginess 79
Allies or Enemies – you decide! 83
  Mindset 83
  Choice 88
  Perspective 91
  Focus 96
  Failure 101
  Fear 104
  Humour 106
  Success 108
  The cost 110
  Time 114
  Inputs & influencers 117
  Consistency 119
  Habits 124
  Work/Activity 127
A moment to pause… 133
Six Benefits of Self-Leadership 135
  1. Controlling what you can 135
  2. Attract high-calibre people 138
  3. Healthy teams 140
  4. Maximising opportunities 143
  5. Making a positive difference 145
  6. Establishing a legacy 147
Why Coaching is Transformative 153
Faith Does Not Mean Perfection 163
Closing thoughts 167
References 173
About the Author 179

CHAPTER ONE

Why this is crucial

Have you ever thought about how well you lead yourself?

I find the element of self-leadership fascinating and challenging at the same time. It is extremely empowering to realise that you can control how you respond, think, and communicate at any given moment. YET, that responsibility means that we cannot blame others and live as victims of circumstances. It is where 'the ideal and reality' wrestle. Adding to that, the selfless focus and the endeavour to become the best expression of ourselves (in any given moment) increase the pressure, BUT the benefits will be discussed later. If you consider yourself to be disciplined, the idea of self-leadership will be more appealing, but there is a successful way to self-lead, however you see yourself. There is always hope, wherever you feel you are right now. With the right inputs and motives, YOU can enhance your life and discover more meaning by maximising your talents, time, and energy through successful self-leadership.

My purpose in writing this book is to encourage and inspire you to pursue excellence in all facets of life. I am confident that this book will provide the essential groundwork needed to support your journey towards excellence. The knowledge you gain from these pages will further empower you to consistently understand, value, and lead yourself well every day, without fail. This will also equip and position you to understand, appreciate, and lead others more effectively. As you do this, it will create a ripple effect, positively impacting your personal life and those you lead. One thing you should know about successful self-leadership is that it is not exclusive to those who are naturally super-organised. However, effective planning and good time management are certainly some of the fruits of practising self-leadership.

I write to those who consider themselves 'semi-successful', having achieved certain significant milestones in life they deem important yet feel restless, sensing there is more to life and more to THEMSELVES yet to be uncovered and expressed. In the following chapters, we will look at various aspects that can sharpen and increase our leadership skills and continue to raise our awareness to become more effective leaders. I believe you have the power and potential already within you to do this. As we journey along, I will highlight different areas to develop, but *you* have to apply them yourself and put in the work to experience the benefits.

You decide whether you are, or become a great leader

Remember, success is less about where you start and more about where you finish. It is more about who you have become and assisted along the way. In the early stages of my personal growth journey, I discovered that the key to my development was not only about challenging my existing beliefs and hearing new things but also allowing what I was learning to take root. It also entails revisiting these things regularly.

I operate from the perspective that living things want to grow; however, I only work with people who want to change their lives. When asked, most people want their lives changed, but only a few are willing to change it themselves. Most just complain about wanting a different life and then continue as they are. But as you read this, I believe you are one of the global minority who are purposeful in their actions and looking to become and do more.

For you...

This content can really benefit YOU and anyone in any stage of their leadership journey **IF** they sincerely want to grow and achieve more satisfaction and significance. Great leadership first aims to make improvements. It is all about being proactive to bring about positive change, and it starts with ourselves by leading from within. Because leadership is recognised more as being visible, 'out there', in public, we can forget that leading others well must start (and continue) with our own self-leadership. It would be hypocritical to try and lead others well without first developing the habit of leading ourselves in a healthy and consistent way. If we attempt this, we imply that we do not see a need or value in leading ourselves well. We can also be suggesting that our behaviour is disconnected from the responsibility and privilege of leading others. NOTHING could be further from the truth!!

>>Think about it for a moment:

What if everyone led themselves well, regardless of their role or position?

What if they focused their time and effort on empowering others to do the same? How different would our societies and cultures be?

Can you think of an area you desire to improve in your self-leadership? *[Note this down]*

CHAPTER TWO

Success is within reach

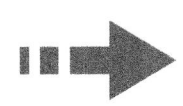

'Reach' implies action and a stretch beyond what you currently have. Wherever we find ourselves at this point, if we are honest, we can all do something more to live and lead better. Whether you are starting your leadership journey, already an accomplished leader, or somewhere in between with your awareness gradually expanding, I want to share that I have been a devoted student of leadership for several decades. Throughout this journey, I have also had the privilege of mentoring and coaching new and seasoned leaders from diverse nations. Based on my experience, I can affirm that the principles and elements essential for self-leadership are universal and timeless. They are the same for each of us despite some cultural variations. We never truly arrive at a place of mastery, regardless of the length and breadth of our experiences. I think this is actually motivating because instead of seeing it as an unattainable goal, we can look at it as an ever-expanding opportunity for personal growth and self-discovery. As a result, it allows us to continually unearth more about ourselves and our capabilities.

I believe we are all leaders, whether we see ourselves that way or not, or have a job title that denotes this. We are *always* leading at least one person… ourselves! I believe it is untenable and counter-productive to ignore this reality. YOU are the most influential contributor to developing your leadership skills, influence, and effectiveness. You are your biggest asset, BUT you could also be your biggest liability!

You lead you.

How many books remain unwritten? How many businesses have yet to start or scale? And how many talents stay unexplored because of people's limited self-leadership awareness or their failure to take action and lead themselves well?

There is a dual focus for this book:

1. Highlighting areas to aid in deepening your insight by developing heightened awareness regarding how well you are currently leading yourself in all aspects of life. As you take personal responsibility to improve this and implement corresponding actions, your life will be more productive and successful. You will experience a greater sense of fulfilment, naturally finding it easier to lead others better.

BUT I am hoping you have the courage and conviction to go to the next level, from success to significance, by:

2. Enabling your leadership to become more about lifting others to new heights of growth, experience, and effectiveness. The question now is, are you willing to go against the destructive nature of selfishness, which is to just serve your own interests and rise to the level of selfless self-leadership?

There are many examples of people leading themselves well and from a selfless perspective. Some are in the public eye, and others just go about their day-to-day lives, making a positive difference to individuals, communities, and the wider world. A lot of the time, selfless acts go unnoticed or unannounced, and that is the point! But there are beneficial times when evidence of these is highlighted to inspire us and nudge our focus back to this higher level of living and leading.

I regularly meet, hear about, and work with people who are growing their self-leadership ON PURPOSE and have the heart to make the world a better place, not just their own lives. I intentionally associate with and try to surround myself with those with this approach. However, I am sure you will agree that whatever stage we are at on our life journey, we all have some capacity to improve in this area, even if just a little! We could all live better. People I lead are better influenced when I lead myself effectively. This is a universal principle that also applies to your life, whether you are conscious of it or not.

The good news is that we all, at some level, have already led ourselves. Using self-control (one element of self-leadership), we tell ourselves *"no"* regarding certain things and make the right decisions that benefit ourselves and others. How do I know? Well, unless you are consuming chocolate 24/7, you have probably drawn upon self-control at some point. You have either put it away or consumed it all without rushing to buy more right away! That is self-leadership, at least to some extent. Recognise these small wins and build on them.

BUT what if we raised our current level of self-leadership so that we intentionally and consistently led well all the time? What sort of difference would that make to your life and those you interact with?

One subject, many facets

Self-leadership has many facets, and these are all interrelated. You will notice in the subsequent chapters that some elements appear in multiple sections. This is intentional to demonstrate how interlinked they are. Like the human body, where various parts work together, an issue in

> You are your biggest asset, BUT you could also be your biggest liability!

one area can affect the performance of several others. Hence, successful self-leadership requires us to develop and operate in many elements simultaneously and to consistently manage them well. A few examples include our health, mindset, skill set, and competence. Therefore, to really maximise your life, it stands to reason that these elements should be prioritised. If we just try to focus on developing one area while neglecting others, we get out of balance. Just imagine the imbalance of developing one bicep and ignoring the other. It would draw attention for the wrong reason!

Hence, the scope of this book covers key factors involved in successful self-leadership. Actions in these areas swing the balance towards them being an ally or enemy to successfully leading ourselves. There are other self-leadership elements outside of this scope: problem-solving, discernment, dealing with conflict, etc. Developing and building on those included here positions you well to grow internally and be effective in these other areas, too.

The most successful leaders are committed to ongoing personal development. The moment we stop growing and learning as individuals, we stagnate and start to regress (because the world is constantly changing and moving forward). I am always looking to expand my knowledge in areas of personal interest, competence, and necessity because gaining understanding will give me an edge. My aim is not to gain an advantage over others but to optimise my life and lead better.

How well do you know YOU?

I ask this because, as you read this book, you will interpret and view the content from the perspective of how you are wired when it comes to your personality type. The DISC Personality Assessment is powerful in identifying and understanding our primary and instinctive personality blend, which affects our behaviour, communication, and so on. That is why I use DISC with leaders to raise their self-awareness, broaden their understanding of those they lead, and know the reasons behind their behaviour.

Note: We all demonstrate the four main personality types that DISC identifies at different times and to different degrees, so one type is not more 'important' or 'valuable' than another. One type does not have more of an advantage to self-lead better than another. Also, do not feel stuck with a particular 'label' if you find this restricting. Discovering your natural personality traits should be liberating, not restricting, because it reminds us that we are not all the same. Hence, our behaviours and thinking will be different at times. For example, something that appears clear to us may not necessarily be obvious to others, and vice versa.

I believe you are reading this because you have recognised that inner hunger, the desire not to remain stagnant but to progress, grow, and expand your potential, thereby expanding your horizons. Here is a sobering thought: if at any point you decide to stop growing, take a mental snapshot of your life at that point and enjoy that moment. Why? Because that is the best your life will be! From that point on, your life will start to shrink, and you will become smaller on the inside (until you decide to start re-investing in yourself and your potential).

Your inner world creates your outer world

To really develop and have the maximum positive influence possible, we need to realise that there is a direct correlation between the extent to which we deal with the internal stuff and the level of success we will experience regarding external things.

You know you could do better at times when it comes to behaviour, thinking, and expressing your emotions, but how can you achieve this and stay consistent? The elements covered in this book are the fundamentals to enable you to do just that. This book is not the magic bullet that, by owning it, transforms you into a great self-leader. Possession of knowledge is just one part of transformation. What truly matters are the day-to-day decisions you make based on these elements, whether you feel like it or not. These choices will make a real difference and set you apart as a great self-leader, and consequently, a great leader of others.

The areas included have universal applications, and I have introduced them with my unique perspective, experience, and the flavour I bring to the world. Some of this content may be new to you and can serve as encouragement that, despite where you find yourself now, you can intentionally make quality decisions to steer and lead your life better from now on. In another light, depending on your growth journey so far, you may be familiar with certain points. If so, these can serve as a reminder of things you have heard but have either forgotten or can utilise to refresh and reinforce. They also act as enablers, helping you to optimise successful areas of your life and leadership even further.

Use it and come back

As with any book, FIND WHAT WORKS FOR YOU NOW! Will you commit yourself to reading and fully engaging with this book? What would not finishing a book about self-leadership really identify about you and your priorities at this point?

(For those that know me well, I say things 'as they are' {but always attempt to do so in the right spirit}. I think it is more efficient and effective that way. Everyone knows the deal, which can empower quicker! So, if my language here is a bit 'in your face', that is all it is. Read on; do not take offence, as I am for your success!).

Give yourself the time and focus to get the most out of each area. Go at your own pace. You are in control of your growth. The book is intentionally laid out in small sections for practical involvement. I have included the '>>Think about it for a Moment' sections to prompt further thought, so ensure you engage with these questions. Ask yourself new questions in these areas, too (and share them with me). If you want to speed-read or finish this book in a particular time, you will be tempted to skip the questions. Sure, you will get to the end of the book quicker, but will you really benefit from what you are reading? Remind yourself of what is motivating you to read this book. If intentional thinking on these aspects is new to you and feels challenging because you have not yet developed in this area, consider focusing on just *one* question from each section. Then, as you revisit the material, catch the others on the next read. Alternatively, you can start by examining one aspect, whether an ally or enemy, that you want to think about first and spend time on those associated questions.

Questions are the pathway to the answers we are looking for

Grab hold of the parts that resonate with you, run with them, and make the necessary changes so they benefit you. Allow these to be expressed uniquely through you, enhancing the flavour you give to the world. Do not get overwhelmed by trying to maximise and incorporate all these principles immediately. Focus on the priorities, pause the rest, and when the changes have become habits and are an established rhythm in your life, return and review other areas you want to focus on. And where you find yourself less effective in certain elements, do not be too hard on yourself. Instead, look at it from the positive perspective that this aspect is now in your conscious awareness. Also, recognise that there are practical steps here you can take to strengthen these areas and enhance your effectiveness. As I said, all of these elements are interlinked to enable successful self-leadership, so developing any of them will position you better to develop the others over time.

>>Think about it for a moment:

Imagine how different your life and leadership will be as you develop and grow your self-leadership. What changes do you want to see:

- in who you become?

- in what you accomplish?

How aware are you of your behaviour, particularly when under pressure?

How well do you recognise and respond to personality styles different from your own?

Is this a cause of frustration, OR do you see them as an added benefit, bringing a different perspective and enabling a wider view of things?

Before I explain more about what self-leadership is, here is a little about my journey…

CHAPTER THREE

Glimpses from My Story

Growth is possible wherever we find ourselves. Becoming a leader and leading myself well were not obvious or evident from birth. Like you, it is an ongoing journey of discovery and the release of potential.

I consider myself more of an introvert, although I regularly 'put myself out there' in social situations when I want to connect with others or bring assistance. My passion for enabling others to feel accepted, inspiring them to grow, and making them more successful initiates conversations and connections, which I would 'naturally' leave to someone else! (Although I do enjoy them once I have started).

I find immense satisfaction and enjoy the challenge of working in a team dynamic (especially when in a leadership role). However, I also value autonomy, as it allows me to advance activities and projects independently. I am happy now with who I am and enjoy my own company, but I regularly need and desire meaningful interaction with others, and I know this is healthy.

Before taking my first DISC assessment, I discovered that I was more introverted because after hosting or attending social events, I would feel exhausted

> Growth is possible wherever we find ourselves.

despite enjoying meeting new people and having interesting conversations. Taking time out alone seemed to recharge my batteries for the next encounter. Since learning more about DISC and my specific personality traits, it has all become clearer! I am naturally happy being 'behind the scenes' and out of the main spotlight (although I appreciate and value times when my purpose is furthered by being more 'public'). The focus now for defining my life is on having more significance in how I serve others than material success, which can be fleeting.

Trouble within…

Growing up, I struggled with timidity, fuelled by low self-esteem (or vice versa). Looking back, this seems bizarre because I knew I was loved, and I have always had a great, supportive family around me. Despite being a very active child who regularly rode my bike and played football in the park with others from my street and nearby areas, I eventually fell into a pattern of comfort eating out of boredom (and probably some underlying frustration at not channelling my energy constructively). This habit eventually caused me to become overweight—not to the level of obesity, but I was 'tubby'. I rarely experienced bullying at school but was picked on occasionally. Being called 'fatty' and comparing myself to other boys with more of an athletic physique also contributed to low self-esteem, and I was usually one of the last to be chosen for a team in PE class.

Back then, I would never have labelled myself ambitious or a leader. I am naturally very calm and laid back, and while this can be a strength, it can also easily produce a level of passivity that can be a hindrance. The plus side of my nature is that I find it easy to follow other leaders when appropriate. (But when I am convinced of the right thing to do, I put my whole heart into it and can be very focused and driven).

For many years, I lived swinging between the categories of individuals who do not really know what they want to do in life, or if they do, they do not believe it can happen. From an early age, I had an interest in drumming. As I approached the time to leave school, my main desire was to be in a rock band, which I mentioned to my careers officer at the time. I am sure she had heard that a thousand times before! But this did not birth in me a desire to further my musical abilities via college or university, so I left school at 16 to 'get a real job' and started working in an office. The plan was to explore the drumming option on the side until I became famous!

To a large extent, I adopted the approach of taking life as it comes regarding my development once I left school. This perspective brings a subconscious frustration, that for me, remained undiscovered for many years. I had embraced a limiting mindset and perspective during my schooling, where, despite doing well academically, I had decided to leave school as soon as possible and that once I left, my learning would cease. Thankfully, this changed over time. During this stage of life, I continued to develop my spiritual growth. However, there was a disconnect in some of my thinking that kept this separate and compartmentalised from sharpening my skills and competencies.

Steps in my leadership journey…

As a self-taught drummer, during my later teens, my creativity was primarily directed towards writing lyrics and composing songs rather than mastering the rudiments of drumming, including the drum roll and exceptionally fast paradiddles! I enjoyed many hours rehearsing and performing in several bands (though more hours rehearsing than performing!). But I never managed to really get traction and momentum with this. My focus and vision for my future differed from those of the other band members. Despite the disappointments and hurt when bands ceased or I left them, it was a productive period in my growth because not only did I realise that you cannot force people to have the same vision as you (they have their own path to follow), it was during this time that my leadership gifting started to become evident and I became conscious of it. It was a great period of learning and developing my soft skills (leadership, communication, navigating relationships, etc.), but I did not intentionally focus on these elements at the time. Being more proactive and initiating came later on.

Looking back now, it is more obvious that I attracted responsibility in various roles within work or while volunteering. I did not seek it out but would regularly be asked to take the lead and be responsible for people and activities. I had been intentional about developing my character and living by my values before my teenage years. However, my level of awareness and intentionality regarding how to lead and become more proactive started to really accelerate in my thirties. There had been a consistent increase before this, but when you really take hold of the reality that YOU are responsible for your level of growth, that is a powerful wake-up call!

Having experienced uncertainty, doubt, and thoughts of wondering whether I could lead, am I really a leader? I understand the frustration many others feel, albeit in different scenarios in life. When I started working at a Risk Management Consultancy, my desire to lead others was strong, but due to the organisational structure and size at the time, the opportunity for this was elusive for a while. As I continued to grow my skills (and leadership experience outside of the organisation), my responsibilities increased, and the role was flexible enough to grow with me. I started leading process improvements and people in certain areas, despite not having a job title to reflect this. After many years, as the company expanded, I started to line-manage staff and the business systems. I have no doubt that my growth outside of the office had a direct correlation with my growth within it.

If you find yourself in a position where you want to lead others but are expected to just 'manage' an area, targets, etc., or have no apparent scope for this within your role, that is the time to take action and create opportunities. Soon after starting my job at the consultancy, I volunteered on a host team at a large church in central London. After a consistent period of proving I was reliable and capable, responsibility found me again. I was asked to lead a team of volunteers, which was the catalyst for me to start expressing my leadership skills at a higher level. I had been somewhat aware of John Maxwell in the years preceding this, so my first action was to read *Developing the Leader Within You,* and subsequently, *Developing the Leaders Around You*. John has been an inspiration, teacher, and mentor in my personal growth and leadership journey since that time.

During a 10-year period, I led teams at church either weekly or for several large arena conferences annually. These service delivery teams varied in size and responsibilities. After a few years, I also took on some operational activities and planning for teams prior to and at arena events. This period brought great satisfaction and development. This is because part of the strategy was to raise and mentor other leaders, not only as a contingency but more from the perspective of planning for growth and scaling up teams for future expansion. This was when I discovered the joy that developing other leaders brings me. I know this is part of my purpose.

> *I believe there are latent leadership abilities in each one of us*

Some are called to handle more responsibility than others, but we all have room to grow and a part to play in making our communities and the wider world a better place. Part of my role now is to work alongside others to discover and develop their abilities, from self-leadership to leading others, while mixing this with healthy self-belief.

Ongoing challenges

One of the ongoing challenges I find in my own leadership, as well as in those I coach and train, is being distracted in the 'doing'. Another is not balancing the right ratio between seeing the big picture of where their business or organisation needs to go and tackling the day-to-day activities and issues that need immediate attention. Heightened self-awareness, intentional life management, and empowering others are key elements to resolving this. Develop strategies and accountabilities, surround yourself with the right people, and commit to a continuous journey of growth and development to keep the main thing, the main thing!

Additionally, people can bring great strength to a team, department, corporation, etc., but usually, the most complicated issues to resolve are people-related. Prioritising the well-being of people (staff, clients, and suppliers) while maintaining balance with operating productive systems and processes requires regular oversight, review and leadership.

Know the areas you find challenging that are not your strengths, and put strategies and processes in place to offset these, accompanied by support from others where required. Delegate and automate wherever possible.

"Our success is hidden in how well we lead ourselves"

CHAPTER FOUR

Defining Self-Leadership

You are ALREADY leading yourself in some measure. But is the term self-leadership self-explanatory? I like to use this definition; it does not encapsulate it completely but makes the point.

Self-leadership is:

'Doing what is most beneficial when you need to do it and choosing to be happy about it!'

If that sounds challenging, think about it this way. If you do not lead your life intentionally—how you spend your time, effort, finances, emotional capital, and so on—someone else will!

More than words

The term 'self-leadership' can make some feel a little uneasy, that the focus is too much on ourselves as individuals, leading to selfish acts. That is a narrow perspective, and I hope that as you read on, the true qualities, benefits, and value of self-leadership will become evident within the right context. 'Personal leadership' is an alternative phrase used for leading ourselves. Again, using 'personal' can suggest that it is solely about your personal leadership, which is not anyone else's concern. However, if you view it from this perspective, you miss the reality that great and effective leadership, when fully expressed, extends far beyond ourselves. Whatever words or phrases you use, just remember that it is definitely about us, but as mentioned earlier, we should lead ourselves well to enable us to THEN lead others better. Everyone benefits that way.

Here are a few of the components of great self-leadership, listed with their opposites:

Positives*	Alternatives
self-love	self-hate
self-lead	self-sabotage
selfless	self-absorbed
self-care	self-harm
self-control	self-indulge
self-expression	self-contained
self-actualisation	self-degradation

*In order to avoid the 'usual suspects' in the second column, focus on developing those in the 'positives' list. These will require regular intention and effort from you, because without them, the 'alternatives' will naturally become evident and grow.

So, how well are you leading yourself in your day-to-day activities, moment-to-moment thinking, and decision-making? Successful self-leadership does not, by itself, solve all of your problems. While it can enable you to avoid MANY pitfalls and challenges you would otherwise encounter, its true value lies in fortifying and equipping you to navigate THROUGH life's different events well. The better you navigate things, the better you are positioned to assist others in doing the same. Having been intentional about consistently developing my self-leadership over several decades, I know this has placed me in a better position to successfully navigate some of the usual suspects common to us all: career changes, redundancy, loss of loved ones, heartbreak, frustration, periods of uncertainty about where we should go next, high-maintenance people, ill health, and so on.

Selfless Self-Leadership

Selfless self-leadership is the highest form of leadership. If our focus is always introspective and channelled towards doing the right thing, I think we have missed the point and trapped ourselves in a world smaller than we should. We are all wired to give and receive love. The best way to experience love is by giving, not receiving it. We cannot successfully lead others if we do not lead ourselves well. If you try to, things will fall apart eventually. However, if our leadership stops at us, so much potential is left undeveloped and latent. Now, writing this book does not mean I have mastered the practice 100%. I still have times when I am a less effective leader. I can get in my own way and focus on what I want, and disproportionately pursue my own happiness. However, as I deliberately grow and raise my level of self-awareness, I become more adept at resisting selfish tendencies. As a result, these instances occur less often and are of shorter moments than before. But at any point, I can choose, either on purpose or by omission, to let my self-leadership slip to a level less than I am happy with! It is at these times that I review what I am or am not doing that is producing the less-than-ideal results, and then make changes.

There are two traps to avoid:

i) not leading yourself well at all—living contrary to your values and dreams, feeling like you have underachieved, or
ii) never letting your focus go beyond your immediate world and what is important to you.

Being selfless does not mean you have to devote all of your time to others, give your money away, slowly disappear as a person, or never get to achieve or possess anything you want. That would not be healthy. You have a rightful place on this planet, with equal value to everyone else, because of who you are, not based on what you can do or achieve. You can still pursue your dreams. Selflessness becomes the filter to check whether your motives and decisions are healthy and balanced. Often, people need assistance in a way that is different from how we would naturally (or comfortably) give it. Are you assisting others how you want to, or how they need it, when there is a difference?

Wisdom is imperative with selfless self-leadership because there will be times when people will try to take advantage of this. Selflessness is a heart stance; do not let others use it to manipulate you into doing something they want you to do when it is inappropriate. I have also discovered that I find it easier to be selfless when I have plenty, whether it is time, money, and so on. The real test is whether I demonstrate selflessness when provision is less apparent.

Living and leading selflessly will sometimes bring discomfort or produce less favourable outcomes for ourselves. But when you view these from a larger perspective, this becomes less of an issue. It seems like a paradox, but the most rewarding experiences we have had often result from serving others.

Evaluate your self-leadership, not by the amount of wealth you amass but by the treasure you place in others' lives

These definitions put things into context:

Selfless – 'caring more for other people's needs/wants than for what you need/want'.

Unselfish – 'not devoted to caring only for oneself; not concerned primarily with our own interests, welfare…'

Altruistic – 'desire to help or bring advantage(s) to others, even if it results in disadvantage to one's self'.[1]

The Selfless Superpower

Our understanding of ourselves, others, and how we authentically express ourselves constantly evolves, but many studies prove that helping others actually benefits us in multiple ways. When we give financially to others, *'prosocial spending'*, we can experience a higher state of happiness than when we spend money on ourselves.[2] When we are *'emotionally and behaviourally compassionate'* towards others, it contributes positively to our happiness, health, and longevity, provided that we do not become overwhelmed.[3] One reason for this is that giving releases the mood-boosting 'happiness trifecta' of chemicals: oxytocin, serotonin, and dopamine. However, these chemicals offer *multiple* benefits to us beyond just making us feel good.[4]

Think about a time when you offered someone assistance, not because you were compelled or forced to, but because you wanted to. It may have been through financial giving or solving a problem they had. How did you feel about it? Was it a positive experience where you felt you contributed to a greater good than your own immediate needs? The next time you give in this way, be purposeful about noticing your emotions. It defies logic that giving something of value to someone else can enrich our life experience, but once you have experienced this, there is no doubt it is true, and you then seek to do this more often. Similar to all things that really bring purpose and value to us, it takes a step of faith to experience it.

Motive

Sometimes, we sabotage the benefits of giving when our motives are wrong or when we begrudgingly give or do something for others. The ideal motive would be to help others regardless of any benefit, but it is also rewarding to know that the by-product of helping others adds positively to our lives. Therefore, when we demonstrate an altruistic approach to leadership, regardless of our seeming losses or disadvantages, the outcome will be beneficial at some point.

Empowering others to be successful

During this season of my life, since starting to write this book, I have been re-examining my actions and 'leanings'. I knew semiconsciously that I possess a natural desire (wiring) to empower others to become more successful, to encourage and equip them on their journey of growth and leadership, but it has become even clearer. I realised again how much joy this brings me. I suspect most people who become coaches share a similar inclination. Coaching, in its purest form, aims to empower others to discover their own answers, and we can also learn a lot in the process. I have now become more intentional about empowering others to be more successful.

Developing a lifestyle of generous leadership exponentially increases your influence because it often triggers generous behaviours in others and increases gratitude amongst recipients.[5] Adopting the golden rule of *'doing to others what you would have them do to you'* keeps our focus outward with a perspective of benefitting those we lead. I generally use the 'be the person you would want to meet' approach, particularly when going into an unknown environment that is likely unfamiliar to others there. I intentionally behave in a more extroverted manner than my natural inclination while still staying authentic. Sometimes, it involves being welcoming, approaching others, starting conversations, and attempting to put others at ease. That not only takes my mind off how I might be feeling but also positions me to improve the experience for those I interact with (or at least, that is the intention!).

You are unique, on purpose!

Although we may grow up in similar environments to our neighbours, peers, and other family members, we all see and interpret the world differently *[see also 'Perspective']*. We all have a unique flavour to share with others. Several people involved in an incident will see it and describe it with variations or in a different light. I believe this is by design. We are all wired differently but predictably different based on the four main personality types identified through the DISC Behavioural Assessment.

You have a great personality. You may be wired in such a way that you like order, processes, details, and structure. There is nothing wrong with that, and equally, there is nothing wrong if you are not! Do you find a perceived 'safety' in having a structure to follow, setting boundaries, and knowing what is 'right' and 'wrong'? If so, you are likely thinking, *'Tell me what I need to do to self-lead well'*. For others, this approach can be too restricting. It can stifle creativity and spontaneity. Their approach is more of, *'Let's explore, collaborate, and discover how to self-lead well together'*. It is important to realise that our journeys, although they may bear some similarities to others, are unique to us. Everyone has their own path to follow. So, any example I share is just that—an example. It is not a hard and fast rule you must follow to be successful; or if you behave differently, you will fail. Not at all. To some of you reading this, you are thinking, *'I wouldn't have interpreted the examples like that'*, which is fine. I am mentioning this to those who would have, and you know who you are!

> Everyone has their own path to follow…

Opportunities to compare ourselves are all around us, but use comparison sparingly. Let it motivate and encourage you, but NEVER condemn you. Comparing our abilities, lifestyle, what we have, how we do things, etc., to others is a double-edged sword. On one side, we can celebrate the likenesses and attributes we see in successful people and ourselves and be inspired. On the other side, aspects that are glaringly different to ourselves and our behaviour can be highlighted, and we can feel ill-equipped, insufficient, or lacking something.

Your beginning, their end

Remember to keep any comparison in perspective. It is easy to look at someone else's success, which may have taken them years of growth, hard work, and building healthy relationships to achieve, and compare it to where we are now. We might be at the start of a new chapter that could eventually lead to something similar or equally successful, depending on our definition of success. However, we have not yet invested the same amount of effort, time, and resources to get there. The start of any chapter of our lives looks way different than the end of it, and it is the same with others, too. Appreciate where you are NOW and who you are NOW. That is who people meet, and that is where you build from.

Simon Sinek writes in *The Infinite Game* [6] about having a 'worthy rival', where we see others in a similar field to ourselves and can use the differences to inspire us to become better at what we do (not to become a clone). You may see specific desirable qualities in someone who is wired differently from you; so to them, these qualities are more instinctive, whereas for you, a lot more effort would be required to produce them. It may be beneficial to develop these qualities yourself, but always approach this from the perspective of what seems more natural for you. Looking at the result of the comparison helps us determine whether it is beneficial. If comparison makes you feel worse, it will likely work against you. If it inspires you to focus more and grow, move, reach out, etc., this is an ally.

Small wins

This can be similar to certain disciplines and habits you see in others that you desire to be evident in your life. But another perspective on this is that you probably have many beneficial habits and life hacks that seem normal; however, when others notice them, it can inspire them to change their behaviour. Your normal may be strange to me, and that is okay. I have heard on a few occasions from leaders in various fields that they have realised the power of incorporating the small discipline of making their bed each morning. Having grown up in a small bedroom, making my bed was essential because, during the day, my bed became part of my workspace, storage place, and sitting place. I also learnt to clear my bed of items before the end of my day, so it is more appealing when I want to go to sleep. This natural discipline, which

I took for granted as normal, others are just discovering, and it is likely we all have something others can benefit from.

Valuing YOU

Your value is in who you are as an individual. It is not based on what you do, achieve, or how well you lead others. All those are by-products of growing your self-leadership. Value your uniqueness and what you bring to the world. We often downplay and undervalue our talents, thinking that 'everyone can do that' because it comes naturally to us. This was a lesson I learnt during band practice in my teenage years when we swapped instruments during a break from playing the same song repeatedly. I knew I could not play the guitar, but I was surprised at the unrhythmic sounds emanating from the drumkit when my fellow members 'had a bash'.

What are you basing your life on? What are the principles, values, and non-negotiables that you live by? If you have not clarified these, I suggest you make time for this to be your next task. Take time to list (or review any you have previously identified) the elements that are valuable to you. Get clarity and be specific about the boundaries you set in your life. Integrity needs boundaries to operate within. These boundaries then provide you with the freedom you need to be the YOU that you want to be. You can use these values to measure how successful you are at leading yourself. The closer your leadership aligns with your core values, the greater the peace, contentment, and satisfaction you will experience. If you are experiencing low levels in these areas, ascertain the root cause and adjust accordingly.

Operating from a place of authenticity and living by your values is the bedrock of successfully releasing what you bring to the

> There has never been a YOU before you; there will never be another YOU after you!

world. Now, that may sound grand, and in many respects, it is! Our talents may not be one-of-a-kind, which is liberating because we need more than one skilled artist, builder, pilot, etc. But expressing these talents through WHO YOU ARE makes them unique. I believe that our talents are gifts bestowed upon us, and we have a responsibility to develop them, not just to serve ourselves but also to empower and benefit others. The level at which we develop and release those gifts will determine the level of our influence.

You are the only YOU on the planet; think about it. There has never been a YOU before you; there will never be another YOU after you! Even twins, despite having a lot of similarities, also possess unique attributes. This is not to put pressure on you, but if you do not have a healthy value of yourself, you will end up living less than you should and short-changing those in your world. Mix that with the wisdom in this quote in *Avengers Endgame*:

> *'Everyone fails at who they are supposed to be. The measure of a person, of a hero, is how well they succeed at being who they are.'* – Frigga, Queen of Asgard (to Thor)[7]

Ensure that humility is the foundation for your self-image to avoid pride growing and sabotaging your efforts. Realise that you are as valuable as everyone else, (but not more so). Let this be inspiring to say *'yes'* instead of *'no'* when the opportunities to grow and express who you are become evident, and motivate you to keep yourself in line and choose great self-leadership.

Your Passion

What gets you out of bed in the morning? What drives you? Why do some athletes start training in the bitter cold of a winter's morning before sunrise? Because they are passionate about breaking a world record or winning a gold medal. Discovering your passion is crucial in the journey of personal growth. There are so many opportunities and directions you can grow in that you have to focus on certain areas. [See also *Focus*]. Aligning your actions and developing habits and routines fuelled by your passion makes life more enjoyable, challenging and productive. It starts to release your potential. You can then take this as far as you want to. Here are some questions to aid identifying your passion:

What are you good at or enjoy doing?
What activities do you do where it feels like time flies by?
What brings a smile to your face while doing it?
What activities feel less like 'work'?
What are you regularly spending money on?

Who decides what great self-leadership is?

Depending on your worldview, you will have qualities you esteem to be great leadership qualities, whereas the person next to you might list different ones. So, who is right? I will leave the definition of great self-leadership for you to decide. You know YOU, and while I understand the value of collating and analysing data to inform initiatives, you know YOURSELF better than anyone when it comes to leading yourself well. As you travel your leadership path of growth and discovery, you will know what great self-leadership for you is and what you would regard as second best.

In these pages, I unpack my perspective and experiences on my journey of discovery so far. I share what has and continues to work for me. Regardless of how successful we see ourselves currently, as we ALL have greater potential to discover and release, I would suggest focusing less on trying to encapsulate a one-size-fits-all definition, as that could limit your growth. There is a tendency in human nature for us to become prideful when we feel we have achieved something. We then use the comparison trap to make ourselves feel better and look down on others. That is the start of a slippery slope to failure.

Personally, I consider Jesus Christ to be the ultimate example of great leadership, both in self-leading and leading others [see also *Faith Does Not Mean Perfection*]. You may have a different perspective and belief. Either way, one aspect that I believe is fundamental to great self-leadership, regardless of a declaration of faith, or indeed the declaration of an absence of faith (if that is not an oxymoron!), is the element of providing help to others (in multiple forms). If we become effective at leading ourselves, only to be found lacking in assisting others, I think we have gone off track *[see also Selfless self-leadership]*.

When your self-leadership is fuelled by a healthy love for yourself and others, this best positions you to learn, grow, and adjust when needed

Things to consider

So, when does self-leadership start? Well, you could say as soon as you awake. Do you get out of bed when you want to OR when you need to (those states rarely correlate from my experience)? Do you lay in bed for a while 'snoozing', repeatedly testing the patience of your alarm clock before arising? Debating and arguing with yourself that, *you really should get up and start the day/it is better to lay here for a few more minutes. After all, if I feel tired, does that not mean I need to rest more?* (Not necessarily, but that is a different topic!). The biological pull can be strong enough to stay there. The phrase, 'listen to your body', is not always applicable.

Or maybe successful self-leadership yesterday could have set you up better for today if you had switched the TV off sooner, or returned home earlier, and gone to bed at a certain time. You could have quietened your mind so that you could drift off quickly. We have all discovered that just laying down with the light off does not guarantee we will fall asleep quickly. The practical, unglamorous elements are the fundamentals we can easily overlook, but keeping these in line consistently contributes to building great self-leadership.

Exposing some self-leadership myths

Myth #1: Self-leadership is all about focusing on myself.

Absolutely not! – Despite cultures leaning more than ever towards self-promotion and self-branding, self-leadership is not all about focusing on oneself. If all your focus, thinking, and growth are just about you, then you are not really having the impact, influence, and significance you want. It *is* important to regularly focus on things about ourselves and our lives and develop in areas where we need to change. For instance, are we utilising our strengths as well as we can? *But then*, let us think bigger than just our immediate world and what pertains to us. If we keep the habit of regularly looking in to then look out, we are more likely to keep a balanced perspective.

Myth #2: Self-leadership is about reaching perfection.

It would be unrealistic and self-defeating to try to achieve perfection. We recognise that no one is perfect, so expecting perfection from ourselves or others (including those in leadership roles) is wrong. There will be moments when you do not act or think as well as you could or want to, but keep these as moments. Once you recognise it, make changes and do what you must to return to intentional self-leadership *[see also Myth #4]*. Quality self-leadership is far from being arrogant and acting like we know it all. It is possible to lead ourselves really well, BUT if we are strutting around in arrogance, thinking we know best, then:

i) We are deceiving ourselves.
ii) We put a distance between us and the people we lead. It hinders trust from being built, and let us be honest, your team know you do not have it all together! They know that you do not know it all!

So, let us be authentic in how we live, lead ourselves, and lead others.

Myth #3: Self-leadership means I have to keep working.

It is not all about 'doing' and working long hours but more of a shift in perspective, realising that intentional growth is constant. As we grow, we tap into that latent potential within us, which is exhilarating because we become more like our authentic selves, which energises us. Now, it does take effort at times to overcome either tiredness or feeling down from failing, etc. These sometimes attempt to rob us of momentum, but once we start taking action to grow, we activate that part of us that really wants to improve. If you still need motivation, picture the alternative to leading yourself well, i.e., missing opportunities, self-sabotaging your potential, not benefitting others, living below par, etc.

Generally, leaders are very active. We like to do stuff, progress things, and always be moving forwards. Leaders in many realms struggle with balance. The more we are responsible for, specifically if we are running our own business or leading a large organisation, the greater the temptation to tip the balance too far. But successful self-leadership is a growth lifestyle where we ensure we have enough rest for ourselves in the process—balancing the activity, growth, and thinking regarding professional AND personal elements, AND scheduling times to 'switch off' and relax. Incorporating acts of self-love and doing things that recharge us is so important. Taking that holiday can be as crucial to self-leadership as implementing a growth plan or starting a new project! *[See also Rest].*

Myth #4: Self-leadership means I cannot make [or admit] mistakes.

It is not about being too hard on yourself when you fail or do less than your best. Be honest with yourself and understand why you are underperforming in that scenario or how you could avoid making that mistake again. I am all for setting the bar high regarding our thinking, behaviour, and productivity, but we must be realistic. We will miss it sometimes, and there is no shame in that. The measure of our self-leadership is HOW we respond when we do.

For many years, I led multiple high-performing service delivery teams of volunteers, with a strong emphasis on empowering individuals and developing new leaders. It is an area of strength for me that I really enjoy, and I find huge satisfaction in being involved in it. Despite this, I made multiple mistakes but took responsibility for them, corrected the errors, and apologised as needed. I owned up to them rather than making excuses, or worse, blaming a team member!

When you are the leader, the buck stops at you, but that does not mean you are an expert at everything. Try to minimise the possibility of mistakes through good planning, resourcing, communication, and surrounding yourselves with others gifted in your less-developed areas (wherever possible). But, when such slips happen, people will respect you much more if you are honest with them. If they never see that you are human, they will find it hard to relate to you, which will hinder the building of trust and working together effectively. Consequently, it will be difficult for you to develop them.

Do not believe these myths, YOU can self-lead well…

EVERYONE has the power to build up or tear down people, to assist in their growth and development, or to hinder them. We can contribute to a downward spiral of doubt, low self-esteem, and unfulfilling actions, OR encourage and inspire them to believe in their potential, develop their strengths, and live better. The question is, which will you choose?

>>Think about it for a moment:

How much of your current life results from being intentional, and what elements are there by default?

What default elements will you intentionally change?

1.   2.   3.

What element will you focus on first?

"Great and effective leadership, when fully expressed, goes way beyond ourselves"

CHAPTER FIVE

Attributes of Successful Self-leadership

All these attributes are attainable for you, and more! This list is not exhaustive. When you see these regularly produced in your life, it is evident that good self-leadership is taking place. Consistency then develops these from good to great. How far do you want to go?

Honesty

It is difficult to overstate the importance and value of honesty. Honesty is the foundation underpinning trust, and without trust, our well-being and relationships suffer. In fact, our influence diminishes. Dishonesty debilitates.

With yourself

We know how important honesty in others is to us, but we should hold *ourselves* to a higher expectation of living and leading honestly. Be honest with yourself. There is no point trying to con or convince yourself that *'I will be a better leader one day'* if you are regularly unwilling to pay the price. Apply yourself, put the effort in to develop this as a lifestyle, and keep moving forward. You either want to experience the fulfilment of personal growth, self-discovery, and the expansion of possibilities through successful self-leadership, or you do not! Suppose you start to give yourself reasons to reaffirm why you avoid taking the higher ground in your actions and decisions. In that case, you begin to descend on the slippery slope to mediocrity, destined to live 'wishing for' instead of experiencing the success you desire, whatever way you define that.

Evaluate yourself on evidence of self-leadership, not intention

The reality is that living honestly always requires intentional self-leadership, which regularly focuses our attention on and allows our defined values to be expressed. Truth fuels honesty, and while individuals may define truth differently, ensure that you operate from the truth you have.

Honesty contributes to our wellbeing, lying does not. There is a natural rest to living honestly, and findings from research by Anita E. Kelly, PhD, at the University of Notre Dame found that '*participants could purposefully and dramatically reduce their everyday lies, and that in turn was associated with significantly improved health.*'[8]

> Dishonesty debilitates.

With others

As we value and cultivate living honestly, we experience a greater sense of peace and inner alignment, enabling trust to flourish. People can rely on us more, thereby attracting greater levels of responsibility and influence. There are multiple opportunities at any given time to choose the dishonest approach or the more subtle versions that live in the 'grey' areas disguised as 'white' lies. There is often pressure linked to these, mixed with the natural desire to avoid having awkward conversations, disagreeing with someone, or confronting an area of failure or bad behaviour in others. Pressure can stem from someone's expectation, a reluctance to stand out from the pervading culture or peer group, a fear of how you would be perceived and treated, etc. If someone asks you to lie for them, and you do this to keep them on your side, you actually undermine the relationship because if you would lie *for* them, they will assume you would lie *to* them.

> \>\>Think about it for a moment:
>
> Can you identify a dishonest area in your life now?
>
> What changes can you make to correct this?
>
> What was/is the underlying driver for compromising honesty in this situation?

Rest

Ensuring we get the right amount of rest significantly contributes to living well and performing at our best. Scheduling regular long and short rest periods ensures we are more productive when we return our focus to activities.

Author Max Frenzel writes, *'Excellent work, particularly of the creative and innovative kind, needs rest and relaxation just as much as it requires time actively engaged in work. When we rest, our brain is busy consolidating memories, and quietly searching for solutions to problems we encounter.'*[9] Author and consultant, Alex Soojung-Kim Pang complements this, *'Rest is not this optional leftover activity. Work and rest are actually partners…The better you are at resting, the better you will be at working.'*[10] Rest will look different for each of us, depending on what we do, what we enjoy, and how we are wired. We can strategically plan rest times rather than waiting until we feel tired or overwhelmed.

Rest is not the absence of activity

For me, this is an area I need to balance regularly. I thrive on activity and always have multiple things I want to work on, so it is easy for me to move from one task straight into another. When you enjoy each activity, you can justify doing this, but I know that I need to set both short-term and long-term boundaries for 'work-related' activities and personal growth. Personally, I find that 'switching off' and engaging in restful activities for a period requires a high level of intentionality from me, but it is worth it, and it contributes to higher productivity when I 'switch back on'.

Throughout the day, I intentionally set short pauses between different tasks. I am also learning to ensure I pace myself, allowing moments to reflect and think instead of rushing into the next activity. As the ancient proverb states, *'...much study wearies the body.'*[11]

> Rest is as much mental as it is physical.

In addition, I always plan one day off per week, ideally the same day each week. I still learn and grow on this day but resist thinking about and partaking in 'work-related' activities. Even though it feels less like work when you are passionate about building a business, offering a service, etc., having a specific, regular day off enables us to recharge, keep balance, add variety, and gain a bigger, better perspective.

Rest is as much mental as it is physical. If you decide to take some time out and lie on a beach to enjoy the heat of the sun and the sound of the sea but continually ruminate about an idea or a next step, this will cause unrest in your physiology. Also, you are not giving your mind an opportunity to focus on your surroundings and enjoy the break from your routine. In addition, this is even more damaging if you are ruminating over something causing anxiety, a misunderstanding, an upcoming unpleasant task, and so on. As much as possible, always be 'present' in your restful environments and resist the temptation to bring agitative thinking and behaviours there. When you successfully rest, you will often find that inspiration will either appear during this time of rest or soon after returning to your focused activities. Pausing to start again more powerfully can seem like a mental contradiction, particularly as many cultures celebrate 'busyness' as a sign of success.

> >>Think about it for a moment:
>
> What environment or activity gives you rest?
>
> Do you have a routine for rest?
>
> How could you make rest times more effective, physically and mentally?

Self-care

Effective self-leadership is not all about productivity but balances self-care well. Self-care comes in many forms and is predominantly about giving yourself what you need and making time for something you enjoy. Self-care is not selfish, although it could be if it becomes unbalanced. Regularly placing yourself in a restful and rejuvenating environment contributes to good health and well-being. It can also include participating in a hobby or activity you enjoy which allows for self-expression and revitalisation. After all, you cannot pour out of an empty cup. It can be tempting to 'try' and fit this in around a busy schedule, but in reality, if it is not scheduled and valued as important as a business meeting or task of responsibility, it will often get postponed and neglected. Do you regularly schedule time for self-care? If not, is this because you consider it less of a priority?

In addition to blocking out set times to recharge, why not allow more time for spontaneous self-expression among your day-to-day activities? This could be as simple as singing along when you hear your favourite song or dancing when no one is watching (or maybe when they are!). Small acts can alleviate stress, keep anxiety away, or just make you feel better, regardless of what you are doing.

Remember not to beat yourself up over mistakes. Give yourself some slack, but not too much space where you allow sloppiness or a bad attitude to grow. A key element is to forgive yourself. If you set your expectations to never make a mistake and always make the right choice, say the right words in the right way, and at the right time, you set yourself up for failure. I definitely recommend defining and setting a standard of excellence for yourself to live by. It stretches and motivates you to grow, but this is different from trying to achieve perfection. You are human. Like it or not, we regularly get things wrong! When you make a mistake, forgive yourself, admit responsibility, and put right what you can. Apologise, heal a relationship, identify an area you need to grow to avoid this from happening again, and take action to start the growth process in that direction.

> The words you hear yourself say are powerful.

The words you hear yourself say are powerful, so ensure that you avoid criticising yourself. Putting yourself down verbally and wallowing in self-pity or self-loathing does not serve you, your purpose, or those you lead and serve. You are WAY TOO VALUABLE for that.

Celebrate the 'small' wins

When you achieve something big or small, celebrate it however you feel comfortable. Tell yourself, *"Well done"*, fist-pump the air, and so on. It is easy to overlook progress and 'small' wins when focusing on the bigger goal. But in order to enjoy the journey more, ensure you recognise and celebrate progress and 'small' successes. This will boost your mood and well-being. It will raise your level of gratitude and awareness of success and when to acknowledge it. This will also sharpen your perception when observing it among team members. Look for something you can celebrate now. Be specific. The more emotionally involved we are in our activities, the greater potential for enhanced performance, and the more easily we will remember them.

Health

We are responsible for our health. Our bodies facilitate us serving our purpose, and they are designed for movement. Avoid sedentary habits by finding ways to exercise and energise your body rather than approach it from the perspective of, *'I suppose I better spend 30 minutes on the treadmill'*. If running on a treadmill does not excite you, go for a hike, take a fitness class, or climb a rock face! If we do not enjoy the energetic activity, it has less of a benefit to our overall health. Discover a healthy pursuit that 'lights you up' and schedule regular time for this. Exercising with a friend or participating in a team sport can be a great motivator because others keep you accountable to show up and participate.

Are you aware of just how important regular and the right sleep duration is to your health, thinking, concentration, and pretty much every other area of your life? Developing your schedule so that sleep is given the right level of priority will contribute to productive longevity.

Regarding nutrition, ensure you find the foods that work for you. Just like the media inputs we permit to influence our thinking and perspective, what we allow into our bodies contributes to the status of our health. Despite something tasting great momentarily while on our tongue, it may be terrible for our well-being. Although a 'treat' occasionally can be positive and considered by nutritionists and personal trainers as acceptable, self-control with food ensures that we avoid comfort eating. Most indulge in comfort eating because they desire to 'escape' or subdue undesirable feelings by replacing them with the temporary mood boost our bodies reward us with when we eat. This quote has been attributed to several people, and we can use it to keep our approach in balance: *'Eat to live, don't live to eat'*.

>>Think about it for a moment:

Look at your calendar. Do you have a leisure activity scheduled regularly, i.e., an art class, team sport, a spa day, attending a book club, etc.?

> When was the last time you celebrated a 'small win'?
>
> Where can you make one change to improve your sleep, nutrition, and movement?

Emotional intelligence (EQ)

What is EQ? We each have the ability to be self-aware, able to recognise how we feel at any moment, and empowered to understand, process, and manage our emotional state well. Strong EQ also means that we are aware of, understand, and can skilfully respond to others' emotions in a positive way. David Walton, in *A Practical Guide to Emotional Intelligence*, states that EQ incorporates:

- Cognitive intelligence – the ability to think rationally, act purposefully, and manage your environment. It is your intellectual, analytical, logical, and rational skillset.

- Social intelligence – the ability to understand and manage situations that involve other people. It is your ability to be aware of yourself, to understand yourself, to manage relationships, and understand the emotional content of your behaviour'.[12]

When recording a podcast episode with Rebecca Laurel-Hill (prev. Schauer), Executive Coach and Registered Dietitian, about her book, *It's Just Food,* she described this succinctly: *'Feeling feelings well is a skill'*.[13] This reminds us that, as a skill, it can be learned and developed. Strong EQ is not the gift of a few, but it is evident in those who have honed this skill. Let this reality really sink in. We can learn to choose how we respond to things, regardless of how we feel.

You are in control!

When you choose how you respond at any point to any situation, you never give the power of your feelings to another person or circumstance. Whether someone is intentionally goading you for a reaction or blissfully unaware that their actions are testing your emotions. Other people cannot make you upset or angry unless you allow them to! Have you ever had someone barge past you as they rush somewhere? Did you take it personally? Chances are they have no clue who you are and are just focused on getting somewhere by a certain time. Of course, it is impolite to barge someone! Yet, their actions have nothing to do with who you are as a person or whether they would like you if they took the time to get to know you. Remember, it is all about perspective!

Emotions reveal the types of thoughts we have, whether positive or negative. Different experiences influence our thinking. Do you catch yourself at times being grumpy? You can choose to stay there or change your state to something positive. When I detect I am getting frustrated, I ask myself, *'Trev, how can you lead yourself better?'* Most times, that is all it takes for me to change, take the higher ground, think of something positive, OR reframe my current reality with a positive perspective.

Experiencing the whole range of emotions is natural and right. We should feel and express our feelings regularly. It is not wrong to have those feelings, but how we express and respond to them will determine our success level. Allow your character and principles to aid you in choosing the right response. Learn to act from who you are and not by how you feel at any given moment. Every day, we choose whether to be happy, downcast, or just mediocre. What will you choose?

Go on, grin!

A simple habit I developed years ago was smiling at myself whenever I looked in a mirror before leaving it. This is not vanity but a visual reminder that I like who I am and am becoming. It also means the last image I see of myself is a happy one. This is a quick mood booster. Try it, even when you are not feeling happy. Do not focus on the aspects you want to change, like hair, wrinkles, and so on. Instead, use it as a moment to appreciate who you are and take control of your emotions.

> We can learn to choose how we respond to things, regardless of how we feel.

Remember also to emotionally enjoy 'now', whatever it holds. The more emotion we mix with our focus, the more engaged we are. You cannot live 'all in' and keep your emotions separate. Neither can you live passively and disconnected and expect to experience life to the fullest. It is good to stay measured about outcomes you have limited control over to avoid unnecessary hurt and disappointment, but you cannot always avoid these feelings. Being emotionally invested connects us to events, moves us into a heightened state (not hype), and helps us see clearer, attracting positive things. If we never risked being hurt, we would never experience love.

EQ in Paris

> A perfect example of EQ was demonstrated years ago while on a family city break. We could each speak French somewhat—not fluently, but we knew the basics. One morning, we decided to buy combined day travel and venue access tickets at the train station. So, on this occasion, we needed more tourist French than *'Un carnet, s'il vous plaît'*. Keen to stretch my language skills, I joined the ticket queue. This is how long ago it was, because there was a lady in the ticket booth. Remember when you went and bought tickets from a person? Now, we were using euros and not francs, so it was not THAT long ago!
>
> So, I queued for the ticket booth, rehearsing my amazing delivery of how I wanted to order the tickets. I was also calculating the total cost to verify that I would be purchasing the correct tickets, and nothing got lost in translation. Then, the guy directly in front of me approached the ticket booth and started chatting with the lady. While rehearsing, I heard their voices rise. By the sound of it, things were not going as well as they should have been. I continued rehearsing. Things then got to a

head, and the guy said something and stormed off. I was thinking, *'Okay, great. This will be interesting!'* My first sight of the lady in the ticket booth was of her looking at the man walking off, and she responded in a raised voice, waving her hands at him. I thought, *'Okay, here we go'*. So, I approached her, and to her credit, she went from speaking in a raised voice, waving her hands at him, to a polite and calm *"Bonjour"*, as she turned to greet me with a warm smile. In a moment, she completely changed her response to him towards me, which made the whole transaction much more pleasant! This was because she managed her emotions intelligently.

Cool down first

I am sure you will be familiar with the advice, *'If you start feeling tense or angry, count from one to ten first before responding'*. I heard Dr. Robi Sonderegger, a clinical psychologist, elaborate more on this. He advised that if possible, remove yourself from whatever the environment or conversation is, which is making emotions rise higher or hotter than what you would like them to be, and then start counting backwards using a three-digit number sequence, i.e., 199, 198, 197. Without going into the science, it forces a different part of our brain to kick in. As we concentrate on counting down in a 3-digit numbered sequence, there is less internal focus on how we feel. It contributes to calming that part of the brain and the emotions associated with our response. It is a way of cooling down, placing us in a better state where we can choose how to respond more intelligently.

EQ is easier when things are going well and life feels good, but how do we measure success on the EQ scale when challenges arise? EQ is an important part of effective self-leadership, but it is only one element. Self-leadership moves you forward, rather than just controlling how you respond.

> >>Think about it for a moment:
>
> When events and circumstances are less than ideal, how successful would you rate yourself at:
>
> a) recognising your emotions?
>
> b) controlling how you respond?
>
> What strategies, methods, or habits have you developed that enable you to control your emotions in times of pressure and high stress?
>
> What could you add to improve how you respond to your environment and to others?

Accountability

This can be a bad word for some who have had bad experiences, but it does not have to be. Being answerable can bring healthy checks and boundaries to our behaviour.

Accountability works on two levels:

- Personal accountability – you are the only person with you 24/7, every day of every year you are alive. When you have the right level of self-worth and self-care, holding yourself accountable is a positive experience because you want to become the best expression of YOU that you can be. Develop the habit of regularly checking in with yourself to ascertain, *'Am I leading myself well?'*

    'Would I recommend this same behaviour to someone else?'

    When you have difficult decisions to make, ask yourself, *'Which approach would be great self-leadership?'*

- Accountable to others – there is great value in holding ourselves accountable to others, especially those with our best interests at heart. For most, being accountable to others in different areas or aspects of life will involve a mixture of your boss or business partner, family, and friends. The level of effectiveness of this will be determined by several factors, including the strength of the relationships, the level of trust, and the measure of natural bias. To really get objective input and accountability, leverage the benefits of a mentor or a coach. They can provide an unbiased perspective while still 'being in your corner' and partnering with you to succeed in the areas you focus on. They will ask you the tough questions, which family or friends may shy away from.

A coaching client in Norway (who in DISC terms is a high 'I', which means he prefers variety over routine) was juggling his time across several of his businesses. As a coach himself with a good level of self-awareness, he knew that he needed to focus his time better, so he intentionally highlighted this and used part of our sessions to hold himself accountable to me to prioritise certain actions. This really helped him to sharpen his focus and utilise his time and effort better, improving progress. [See also 'Why Coaching is Transformative'].

There is something powerful about hearing ourselves say something to others that we want to be held accountable for. We can have ideas and thoughts floating around in our minds, but when we speak them out in a way committed to progress, we establish these things

> When you have the right level of self-worth and self-care, holding yourself accountable is a positive experience.

and solidify them more in our consciousness. But as you speak these out, listen for your inner voice to check how this aligns with your words. If you find yourself making a statement committing to do something by a specific time, etc., but you hear your inner voice subtly state, *'I'm not doing that'*, be honest with yourself and whoever you are talking to. This reveals a misalignment, and deep down, you have resistance to this for some reason. Save yourself time by realising this and 'owning up' to the reality that this is just a stalling tactic, then adjust or explore more to find the root of the resistance. It is in your own best interest to do so!

> >>Think about it for a moment:
>
> How often do you hold yourself accountable for your actions?
>
> Can you identify two or three appropriate people in your world who will hold you accountable? Those who have your best interests at heart, who will be honest with you, and who will have no selfish motive.

Self-control

'He who is slow to anger is better than a warrior, and he who controls his temper is greater than one who captures a city.'[14]

Self-leadership is more than self-control, although this is a key ingredient to success. Self-control is a spiritual force, so it is stronger than willpower. It equips us to resist temptations that compromise our values. In resisting temptation, self-control is strongest when we use it to avoid getting into tempting situations in the first place rather than calling upon it once we are experiencing temptation.

Do you struggle to control your thinking?
Do you get distracted often?
Do you lean towards inactivity or find it difficult to make wise decisions?
Do you often find yourself in environments that challenge you to compromise what is important to you?

Operating in self-control is not always easy, but developing the habit of resisting certain actions and opportunities and controlling your emotions makes it a little easier to resist the next time. It is like developing a muscle. The more you exercise it, the stronger it becomes.

Oftentimes, even when it is within our capabilities to do certain things without compromising our values, taking a strategic look beyond the scenario and present moment often reveals that it may not be the best option. In such cases, we can choose a better way to behave. This is where emotional intelligence fortifies self-control.

Chemistry Control in Cyprus

> While on holiday in Cyprus with a friend, a lady staying at our hotel caught my eye. There was instant chemistry, and I got the impression the feeling was mutual from a few passing glances. I am generally cautious and logical by nature, so I kept my distance first to think through some practicalities before making contact and to test my heart. I have never been an advocate of 'holiday romances', coupled with a decision I made long ago that a long-distance relationship was not desirable for me. I did some subtle 'research' and ascertained that we did not seem like a 'good fit' despite the attraction. *[I will omit further details here!]*. Most importantly, there was an uneasiness inside about moving forward. Hence, the wisest approach was to avoid direct contact and not look to start the process of getting to know her—despite the 'buzz' chemistry with the opposite sex gives!
>
> (I realise that to the romantics reading this, you may perceive this as a missed opportunity, but for me, I had previously learnt that great chemistry is not enough to build and sustain a long-term relationship. Although I would not try building one where chemistry was absent!).
>
> It, therefore, seemed that the likelihood of success for anything long-term was extremely low. So, I chose to politely keep a distance and not make contact. I really had to keep my thinking and emotions in check for the whole

period we were at the hotel. This is because despite the feeling of unrest inside, it would have been effortless to suppress this, live in the moment, act on the chemistry, and allow something to develop that would actually become a 'distraction' for both of us from ultimately who we are supposed to be with. Besides, it may eventually end in a whole heap of hurt! Emotions can serve us well, but there are times when we should make decisions outside of emotions. These are the moments where choice is critical. I wanted to and did not want to, both at the same time. It would no doubt have been fun in the short-term, but this would have soon passed. I therefore chose the *'do what you need to do and be happy about it'* approach!

Not everything the heart longs for should be followed

Sow what you want to grow

Early in life, I appreciated the value and saw the benefits of discipline and self-control. However, it was not until I first heard the term 'self-leadership' that it all seemed to fall into place. Many of the spiritual principles I had intentionally been developing and demonstrating became obvious because these were leadership traits growing within me over a prolonged period. We have the power to decide what we will sow and invest in our lives and what we will starve. The more consistently we sow the right things, the stronger their root and resilience when adverse circumstances come against us. These will be a source of inner strength that we can draw upon to navigate the unpleasant and unknown.

> We have the power to decide what we will sow and invest in our lives and what we will starve.

Areas we purposely neglect lose their power because what we stop feeding dies. The less intentional we are about what we receive and accept into our thinking, lives, etc., the more control we surrender to outside forces, opinions, and influences, which can diminish our potential. Environment is an important aspect in determining growth, too. You may be sowing good things into your mind, but if you do not manage your inner world and control what you give thinking time to and exclude thinking about, it will not be the most conducive environment for these things to grow.

> When my sister and I were very young, we were each given a small, designated garden patch to grow what we wanted. We could manage it ourselves. Because that was ours and we were responsible for it, we took more interest in it and learnt that what you sow grows. Being intentional about what you put in the ground helps to control what grows and brings delight and reward when it becomes healthy and established. Now, sometimes, things that we did not sow also grew and took some of the room and nutrients from the ground, so it had to be managed well. Regular supervision of what is going into the ground and springing up enables us to maximise the potential of the soil. It is the same for us. Growth is a natural law, but what we allow to grow in us is up to us.

It tastes better!

Since hearing from a few respected sources regarding the benefits of 'mindful eating', I started to develop this practice. When I am alone, I usually sit quietly while I eat, free from distractions and external input. I focus on being present in the moment and on the flavours and textures of the food. This can be challenging and takes self-control, because at any moment, at any meal, I have the opportunity for my mind to wander. Particularly during breakfast because in the morning I am always keen to jump into the day's activities. I must overcome thoughts of, *'But you could be reading or watching something while eating to utilise the time better...'* However, if I do not feel that I can spend 10 – 15 minutes eating breakfast mindfully, my approach to time and activity is surely unbalanced! Not all my meals are 'mindful'. When I make time for this during any meal, I taste and enjoy the food more, which prompts gratitude and improves my digestion. This also develops the discipline of focus. Closing your eyes while doing this can help, but it might appear a bit strange and potentially unsafe when you are dining out!

Exceptions during mindful times are the unpredictable events that arise and need my focus and attention. I will only use my phone during this time to take an urgent call or when I get inspired and want to capture an idea or thought. It was during a breakfast that I captured this point!

> >>Think about it for a moment:
>
> What are you or have you been intentionally growing within?
>
> Are there attitudes, thoughts, and beliefs that you need to stop feeding so that they diminish and die out of your life?
>
> What new elements will you focus on growing?

Reflection

Reflection enables us to see ourselves and our experiences better. John Maxwell states that it is not experience that is the best teacher, but evaluated experience.[15] Leaders reflect on the past, assess the present, and look within to lead into the future.

Making time in each day that I live to regularly reflect on my accomplishments, experiences, feelings, and what I am learning is a challenging area for me. I avoided this for a period until I realised, for my own benefit and others, I had to confront this perspective. Once I discovered the value of reflection, how it could help me stay focused, hold me accountable, and enhance my ability to learn from the past in order to improve the future, it inspired me to set aside a few

> Reflection enables us to see ourselves and our experiences better.

moments at the end of each day. I also dedicate ~twenty minutes at the end of each week, and similarly, at the end of every month and quarter for reflection.

Building this routine is a 'work in progress' for me, as I still find moments when this gets squeezed out of my focus, but linking it to the habit of gratitude has a mutual benefit because it reminds me of things that I have now, things that I have done, and things I can be thankful for. Before I started to reflect, I could easily get caught up in day-to-day activities and become oblivious to trends appearing in my life (good or bad). How can we evaluate whether we are leading ourselves well without pausing to assess our thinking, behaviours, habits, results, etc.?

I use questions to prompt my reflection. Over time, as I gain more clarity, some of these questions change. If this is not a discipline you have developed yet or have let slip, use these example questions to begin with and write your own in due course:

Daily:

- What has made today successful?
- How do I feel?
- What have I viewed as negative?
- How have I grown and what have I learnt today?
- How have I assisted or empowered others today?

Monthly:

- What are the top three priorities this month?
- What accomplishments are linked to these?
- What have I learnt from these?
- What new actions do I want to implement?

Quarterly:

- What is my best accomplishment this quarter?
- Have my accomplishments this quarter contributed momentum to my priorities?
- If not, why?

- What is my highest priority to focus on going forward?

Neglecting self-reflection robs us of valuable insights and opportunities for continuous improvement

Reflecting also has benefits after meeting someone new, having an important conversation, or directly after a meeting. How beneficial would you find it to develop the routine of setting aside 5 - 10 minutes after a meeting to ask yourself:

- What actually just took place there?
- Did we cover all the points to the level required?
- What were the key responses?
- What were the non-verbal cues that I was picking up from the team?
- What was the emotion or feeling of the team?
- What areas were counterproductive, and how can I address them?

You may discover that there are actually a few conversations you need to have just to check that certain individuals are okay and that they understood what you were discussing. If they have objections, consider how to explore them in more detail because you may learn something from how they see things. *[See more on Reflection in 'More of Less'].*

>>Think about it for a moment:

Do you currently have a routine to reflect on your accomplishments and experiences?

If not, how could you explore starting to benefit from this?

[Using the example questions could be a good starting point].

"Everyone fails at who they are supposed to be. The measure of a person, of a hero, is how well they succeed at being who they are"

CHAPTER SIX

Outright Enemies of Successful Self-Leadership

Knowing your enemy gives you the advantage and informs your strategy to avoid or reverse self-sabotaging thoughts and behaviours. Overlooking these elements will seriously hinder your success and effectiveness.

Procrastination

Defined as *'the act of delaying something that must be done, often because it is unpleasant or boring'*.[16]

Procrastination can be sneaky. Others can identify our procrastination quicker than ourselves. We can side-step triggering our awareness that we are actually putting an important activity off by providing 'sensible' reasons to ourselves (and others), i.e., *'it is not the right time'* or *'I'm not quite ready'*. Coupled with the thought, *'I **will actually do** this because it is important…just not yet'*. I discovered during a session with my coach that I had been doing this with regard to preparing appropriate answers to some key questions I would be asked. While there was not a pressing need to complete them immediately, there was a benefit to tackling this activity sooner rather than later. But because I had not ruled out completing the task, it slipped under my 'procrastination radar', which is usually very effective!

> We have the power to change our behaviour.

Has procrastination become a habit for you? Are you allowing your emotions to influence your motivation? Do you only focus your time on the enjoyable elements of life and avoid the unpleasant tasks or those you consider difficult? Regularly delaying or putting off indefinitely important tasks is an enemy to great self-leadership. It creates a cycle of ineffectiveness because it increases stress and task intensity, leading to mental fatigue (where we are more likely to procrastinate even more!),[17] affecting health and well-being. The more we ruminate and think in circles about things, the less room we give ourselves for new ideas, which limits progress and hinders creativity.

Procrastination also makes you a bottleneck and unreliable to those you lead, which complicates and hinders your team's effectiveness and does not utilise time and energy effectively for you or them. I believe we are all created with an inherent desire to achieve, create, or build something, which contributes to experiencing purpose. So, living in a way that postpones achievement restrains the development of healthy self-esteem. We become our own worst enemy. We have the power to change our behaviour.

Now, there may be certain legitimate scenarios where you pause or postpone activities. Just ensure this is a conscious, thought-through decision that serves you well. List out a few reasons for not starting these yet, and then review these reasons after a short time or the next day. Then ask yourself, do they still carry the same weight?

Here are a few of the main culprits, along with some strategies to eliminate their effects:

OUTRIGHT ENEMIES OF SUCCESSFUL SELF-LEADERSHIP

Culprits	Symptoms	Strategies to overcome
Perfectionism (fear of criticism/failure)	We delay starting something until we believe we will have enough time to complete the task. Unrealistic expectations of ourselves. Feeling inadequate.	Change your mindset – your value as an individual is not based on your level of achievement or never making a mistake. Face your fear – identify what you are actually afraid of.
Lack of motivation	Waiting to feel like doing the task. Confusion, lethargy. Unclear of purpose for doing a task.	Feelings follow; just decide to start! Momentum can trigger motivation. Think of the benefits of completing the task(s). How good will it feel to accomplish these? You could also line up a treat for yourself when the task has been completed, or several interim treats linked to stages of progression.
Boredom	Negative perspective; does not see benefits of the task.	Focus on the benefits. Think about how you could make the task more interesting. How could you approach it in a different way? Involve others and utilise a different resource. Make yourself accountable to either a

		daily task list, or if you need more accountability, to a friend, colleague, or coach.
Distraction	Starting multiple tasks unnecessarily. Slow progress or stalling of tasks. No achievement or tangible results.	List priorities and schedule/ring-fence non-negotiable timeslots to progress these. Set clear deadlines for specific steps and milestones. Utilise the Pomodoro Technique or other time management tools. Limit notifications and controllable interruptions.
Overwhelm	Thinking: *'I don't have enough time to do this, so I won't start yet'.* *'I have too much to do.'*	Break your goals and tasks down into small steps or chunks of time. Or go smaller: aim for 'slivers' of activity, not chunks. Each accomplishment gives you a boost, leading to positive emotions that can build momentum. Starting can put things in a better perspective. Required activities may appear less insurmountable once the first step has been taken.

> >>Think about it for a moment:
>
> Can you identify a situation, task, or conversation that you are procrastinating on at the moment?
>
> (To help answer this, list out a few 'tough' things that need to be done but for which you lack motivation).

Lack of awareness

Lacking awareness and insight keeps us thinking and operating at a lower level than we should. How often do you think about what you think about? I remember first *really* realising the power of awareness during my early days of personal development while watching a video by the now-late Bob Proctor. We all operate at some level of awareness, including conscious insight, self-awareness, and awareness of external environments and opportunities. However, it is only when we realise the potential to expand this awareness, become dissatisfied with our current limits, and take actions to enhance it, that we can truly gain more insight into who we are and how we could operate better. Listening to Bob made so much sense, and yet, I knew this was more than just my head going, *'That makes sense. I guess I knew that already'*. No, something shifted in my thinking and belief at that point.

Awareness is fluid. It ebbs and flows, so being intentional about raising our awareness level and consistently operating at that higher level is a key

> Thinking is the beginning of change; awareness is the catalyst for action.

contributor to successful self-leadership. You could be living under the influence of constraining beliefs and old habitual thought patterns that are now irrelevant to who you are and where you want to go. Alternatively, you can be surrounded by great leaders and still be limited in what you can learn from them if your awareness of leadership is low.

Thinking is the beginning of change; awareness is the catalyst for action. How aware are you of the results your current behaviour and thinking are creating for you and others? What influence does your communication have on those you lead? A team leader (who in DISC is an 'I') mentioned that he had realised he often communicates too much detail before making his point. Now that he is aware of this, he has started to make changes to improve his efficiency and clarity when he speaks. Before this reached his conscious awareness, the lack of insight stopped him from taking action to improve in this area. Eventually, it hindered him and his team. With the teams I lead, I remind myself of the requirement to build my awareness of how each member is different from the others, what motivates them, and how they naturally communicate and like to be communicated to. When we lack this insight about them, we will use one communication channel (our preferred one) and assume they are all motivated by the same things that motivate us. You can see how limiting this is!

We will not change what we are not consciously aware of

A lack of awareness is an enemy to our growth and development because, in certain areas, *'we don't know what we don't know!'* At this stage, we operate in what Burch's *'4 Stages of Learning Model'*[18] succinctly describes as 'unconscious incompetence'. Getting external assistance, opening ourselves up to new ideas, and being in an environment of growth all help to mitigate this and move us to the desired level of 'unconscious competence'. It is one of the reasons I enjoy coaching other coaches because, usually, they are already operating on an 'above average' level of awareness as they look to develop themselves further. Although measuring awareness is subjective, I listen to the words they use and look at their results to gauge this.

We can all start to increase our awareness, and the easiest first step is to stop and examine or ask where we are, then embrace what we discover and use this as the basis to formulate change. Failing to do this imprisons our potential.

> >>Think about it for a moment:
>
> Where is your current level of personal awareness hindering you the most? *[An area where you feel stuck]*
>
> What first step can you take to explore raising your conscious awareness in this area?
>
> How can you gain more insight into the motivations and communication preferences of those you regularly interact with or lead?

Limiting beliefs

The question to ask ourselves is not, *'Do I have any limiting beliefs?'* Rather, it should be, *'What current beliefs do I have about _____ that are actually holding me back from _____?'* [fill in the blanks].

Limiting beliefs set imaginary boundaries on where we can operate or how much we can do, which constrain us. Identifying and disowning limiting beliefs really came to the fore in my conscious awareness while training to be a coach. Despite the phrase being seemingly self-explanatory, how often do we recognise those inner beliefs that regularly influence and restrict us?

Limiting beliefs are extremely subtle and easy to hear, collect, and hold on to. However, they are difficult to perceive and replace (particularly if we try this ourselves). It can be done, but discovering them for what they are is a lot quicker and more thorough with external assistance because these beliefs are part of our current operating system and shape how we interpret the world around us. They become lodged in our subconscious minds. At this point, they have an ongoing influence on us until we recognise, confront, challenge, and replace them, if we ever do! We can live with these without any conscious involvement from ourselves, but they affect our feelings and behaviour (determining our results). That is why they are so dangerous and can really paralyse our actions in certain areas.

Guarding the inputs and influences in our lives lets us filter out and minimise adopting some *[see also Inputs…]*. However, the options and opportunities are endless, and other people close to us can suggest or insinuate some. So, we also need to develop our self-awareness, regularly gain insight into whether our behaviour aligns with our core beliefs and values, and detox from any wrong beliefs that try to infiltrate our minds. I want to be able to say that once you have identified and replaced limiting beliefs that it is 'job done', sit back, relax, and enjoy the rest of your life without limitations, but alas, that is not the case!

Unconscious bias

Recognising when bias influences our decisions and thinking is the first step to changing it. And it starts with us. We can justify to ourselves why we are doing or not doing certain activities. We can also find excuses for handling a relationship issue a certain way when, in reality, we really just do not want to admit that we could make a change and lead ourselves better in this regard. Being honest with ourselves can be a big challenge, especially if we are still broken or hurt in a certain area regarding self-confidence or self-belief. But honesty is the best form of self-care. Are you being too lax with your behaviour? Would you accept this if you saw it in someone else? A good way to start to discover the unconscious biases we operate by is to ask ourselves, 'Why…?'

'Why do I think this is acceptable?'

Or,

'Why would I not put in extra effort?'

(You could adopt the '5 Whys' approach used within Lean methodology to really dig down and uncover the less obvious culprits).[19]

Unconscious bias can also affect how we lead others and can take many forms based on, for example, perceived beauty, age, strong rapport, commonalities, gender, ethnicity, the

> Honesty is the best form of self-care.

halo effect, and so on. Pause and evaluate a likely scenario, which team member was chosen for a specific task or role, and why? Are they more approachable but less competent for the required task? Do you perceive them as more suitable based on the area they grew up in?[20] Conversely, we can also be restricted from certain opportunities and a 'victim' of other people's limiting beliefs.

Stereotypes can be limiting beliefs and biases too, which get reinforced as true the more they are adopted. Stop and think for a moment; how would you answer these?

- Men are less inclined to _____
- Women are better equipped to _____
- Extroverts mainly _____
- Generation Z predominantly _____
- Builders are likely to _____
- The British rarely _____

What is the basis for your responses, and why?
Can you see how limiting these stereotypes can be?

Recognising a limiting belief

Have you ever noticed that it is easier to recognise limiting beliefs in others by listening to what they say and observing their actions? The flip side of this means that it can be easier for others to recognise them in us because they are not trying to justify keeping them! Working with a coach can be one of the quickest ways to identify them, but we can also self-coach to some extent. Look for words and phrases used negatively by your inner voice. Words like 'can't', 'never', 'always', 'if only'. Our beliefs become more evident in the words we speak out loud, too. This is why we should ensure that those we associate with most are also on a growth journey. We can encourage each other to recognise unhelpful beliefs.

In a session while coaching an experienced business owner in the USA, as he explored a new venture, he listed out several steps he thought he would have to take in preparation before starting: documents to prepare, researching 'XYZ', conversations to have, and so on. This would have delayed taking the initial step of connecting with a potential client. While I advocate for good preparation, in this instance, thinking that he had to do all of this *first* was limiting his ability to be proactive in building a relationship. It was definitely a 'light bulb' moment when I questioned if each of those things was necessary (or the highest priority), and he realised, *'Actually, no, I don't need to do any of them at this point to make contact'*. This was not actually procrastination in disguise. It was just a limiting belief that he had embraced without challenging it.

We need to treat limiting beliefs as a disease and be resolutely vicious in our approach to rooting them out. Here are some examples to aid the initial process of discovery. How many of these (or variations) do you find yourself currently living by?*

'I can't do anything until I have a coffee in the morning'.
'I'm not a morning person'.
'It's always the same; whenever I _____, this happens…'
'If only I had studied _____, I could have _____'
'If I was younger…'
'You need to have had _____ to be able to _____'
'I just don't have the time'.
'They're too busy to ask'.
'That's just the way I am'.
'I've always done it this way'.
'They may be able to, but I can't'.
'It's different for you'.
'There is no way they would_____'
'I'd be lost without _____'

There may be genuine and appropriate uses of these phrases, but under further examination, oftentimes, they are unlikely to be completely accurate and fixed.

Once you have identified a few, do not be hard on yourself when you do. They are a part of life that we all have to navigate. Challenge your thinking regarding these by asking questions like:

'Why do I believe that to be true?'

'What if I did _____ instead? Would that be so bad?'

'What if changing this to _____ was actually beneficial because _____ ?'

'How would I act differently if _____ happened instead?'

Developing the exercise of pausing all the reasons something would or could happen if..., and thinking from an exploratory perspective of, *'If there were no limitations, what would I do? What could I achieve?'* enables us to dig beneath the surface reasons that our current beliefs tell us and actually looks for ways that, if these beliefs were untrue, we could do '…XYZ'. Invisible does not always mean impossible.

What if?...

Impossible is waiting for you…

Picture what type of effective leader you want to be, then increase it and make that image even bigger. Let your imagination push through your current belief limits and start seeing yourself from this perspective (regardless of any reasons that may surface as to why you could never become this). What if the apparent constraints holding you back in an area were not actually there? Or if they do exist, they may actually be further away than you realise, which means you have more room to operate in and expand before you find resistance. Persistently push back on perceived resistance in areas where you want to progress to find where the current limits are.

Throw me another lemon

While learning to read faster, I discovered that juggling is a good way to develop our peripheral vision (thanks to Jim Kwik). I had never been able to juggle, and the belief about this stemmed from a brief, failed attempt when I was a child, at which point I determined that *'I can't juggle'*. Now, up until this point, I had not seen the benefit of learning to juggle. Hence, I did not feel limited by this belief. But once I discovered this would be a useful skill to develop, more than just a party trick, I decided that I *could* learn how to juggle and started to practise. As I write this, I have just successfully thrown three balls simultaneously and caught them. I believe these are small steps in the right direction. My belief had changed, so my actions corresponded and are bearing positive results.

> >>Think about it for a moment:
>
> What current belief hinders you the most from growing and progressing in the areas you desire?
>
> What is the first step you can take to replace this belief with one that empowers you?
>
> How can you explore finding where the current limits or constraints are rather than where you perceive them to be?

Being unteachable

The root of being unteachable is usually linked to pride. When we assume we know everything about an area or topic, OR when we look at an individual and judge that we are better or more knowledgeable than them, we become inflexible and eliminate the opportunity to learn. Sad to say, but I have been surprised by some of the people I have learnt from because I first judged their outward appearance or success in life before realising my error. Have you ever randomly picked a chocolate from an unfamiliar box, not knowing what the filling was, and been pleasantly surprised by the taste? Sometimes, an extremely valuable treasure is wrapped in unexpected packaging and hidden in the most unlikely places! Gold is rarely found lying on the surface. Are you missing out on learning something valuable because of who you perceive as intelligent and who you consider not to be?

The more open we are to learning, the more we will attract the right next steps. Topics and people we were previously unaware of become visible and start to appear on our radar. Some of this is due to the Reticular Activating System (RAS) in the brain, and some is undoubtedly a result of social media algorithms! I have discovered that while exploring a particular area of learning and growth, I start to see certain individuals, experts, who have been teaching on the topic for years, sometimes decades, regularly appearing across platforms and inputs I give time to. *'When the student is ready, the teacher will appear' [this links with Maximising opportunities].* Some opportunities wait for us on a certain path, which if we do not take because we are closed off to learning, we will not encounter (or at least not in the most optimal time or way).

Another reason we become unteachable is the fear of being taken advantage of because learning makes us feel vulnerable. This fear is particularly prevalent among those with a high 'D' personality (Re: DISC Personality Profiles[21]). Still, nobody naturally feels comfortable being vulnerable because our inherent self-preservation instinct is always guarding us. Remember that EVERYTHING you currently know, you learnt somehow. We share a commonality across the globe: when we are born, even though we have certain leanings, giftings, or natural abilities in a few areas that differ from the majority, we ALL start our learning journey at the moment of day one!

> Sometimes, an extremely valuable treasure is wrapped in unexpected packaging and hidden in the most unlikely places!

Adopting the approach that wherever you are, you can learn something and everyone can teach you something positions you well to be attentive and open to discovery. As a result, you can benefit from the value that each of us carries.

>>Think about it for a moment:

What change(s) do you need to make to enhance your growth journey?

Who have you closed yourself off from learning something from?

What teaching inputs, channels, and individuals could you make room for?

Distraction

Attention has become an increasingly valuable commodity since the explosion of media avenues and access to information. Distractions, by nature, draw us *away from* something *to* something different and are often an unwanted journey that we take by inadvertently allowing our attention to be 'hijacked'. (Although sometimes they are a desired escape). Distractions come in all shapes and sizes. They can be internal or external, subtle or obvious: emails, phone notifications, news alerts, noises in or outside our immediate environment, ideas and inspiration, voices and conversations within earshot, cramp or discomfort, hunger, memories, and so on.

We have the power to choose what we give our attention to. What are you choosing? Do you struggle with spinning too many 'plates', keeping lots of activities going, frequently switching from one task to another, or having multiple simultaneous inputs or interruptions?

> We overcome distractions through recognition and decision-making.

When I am under pressure with many different tasks to complete, particularly if I find some tasks less motivating, I can easily slip back into jumping from one activity to another. I realised that the dopamine boost I received when starting something new made this appealing in the short term. But multitasking kills focus and flow[22] and reduces our efficiency because our brain has to keep switching back and forth to focus on different things. Resuming a task we started earlier means putting ourselves back in the right frame of mind, refreshing the details, etc., which we are certainly equipped to do, but it takes extra time and cognitive effort. This might only be minimal each time, but it will compound if we allow ourselves to be regularly distracted. *[See also Focus]*. I discovered that inspiration and ideas come at the most 'inconvenient' times. In order to value, develop them, and minimise being distracted, I note them down to look at during a more 'convenient' time. I have discovered that if I ignore them or continue with a task, hoping to remember them later, I usually forget them.

Distraction test

We overcome distractions through recognition and decision-making. How perceptive are you at recognising opportunities to be distracted from your priorities and responsibilities? Are you allowing yourself to be distracted to avoid admitting that you are procrastinating, or are distractions arising from someone else—intentionally or unintentionally?

It would be unrealistic to expect not to be interrupted sometimes, but being proactive and communicating clearly can minimise distractions and manage relationships and expectations well. Blocking out time for specific tasks and informing team members that, unless there is an emergency, you will be unavailable during the set time and will address any questions afterwards (or direct requests to another person) is often sufficient.

Testing yourself in this area by examining a portion of your day or activity will enable you to assess the level of distraction present and your inclination for quick dopamine boosts by task switching. Ask yourself:

- How many tasks did I start and complete or progress sufficiently during this time?
- How many distracting opportunities did I avoid?
- What distractions (if any) did I follow?
- Why were the distractions I followed appealing? (The driver behind my behaviour).
- What did the distractions rob me of?
- Was a specific distraction actually helpful?
- *[You could also take the helicopter view [see Perspective] and imagine what your time and behaviour looked like outside of yourself.]* Would an onlooker evaluate your behaviour as focused, productive, or prone to distractions?

Time management tools, strategies, and goal setting are powerful weapons against distraction. Effective self-leaders always have a goal(s) they are working towards, and it is linked to a vision. Intentional, specific goals aligned to a destination (location or state of being) pull us in a desired direction, giving us specific elements to focus our time and attention on to realise the vision and higher purpose we are living for.

>>Think about it for a moment:

Complete the Distraction Test exercise to aid awareness. Choose a particular time period, e.g., morning. Check in with yourself every 60 minutes during the test period using the example questions, and note your responses to see if or how many times you were distracted.

What did you learn from your notes?

What changes will you make to improve your focus and productivity?

Did you contribute to distracting others?

Selfishness

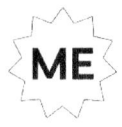

Selfishness has to be the ultimate villain and is usually the elephant in the room regarding leadership. It is a constant struggle if you are alive, (and particularly within the leadership context), because by default:

i) We believe our way is right, which is often underpinned and influenced by confirmation bias.
ii) We naturally think of things that benefit us first. It can taint everything we do by shifting the motive from what is best overall to what is best for ourselves!

I think this extract from The Message Bible[23] encapsulates it well.

> *'It is obvious what kind of life develops out of trying to get your own way all the time: repetitive, loveless, cheap sex; a stinking accumulation of mental and emotional garbage; frenzied and joyless grabs for happiness; trinket gods; magic-show religion; paranoid loneliness; cutthroat competition; all-consuming-yet-never-satisfied wants; a brutal temper; an impotence to love or be loved; divided homes and divided lives; small-minded and lopsided pursuits; the vicious habit of depersonalizing everyone into a rival; uncontrolled and uncontrollable addictions; ugly parodies of community'.* – Galatians 5:19-21 (MSG)

The existence of blind spots means that we can be the last to realise or recognise when this approach has taken the driving seat. If you are reading this and thinking that you do not have a blind spot, then that is a blind spot! As with limiting beliefs, the question we need to ask ourselves is not, *'Do I have any?'* but *'Where do I have them, and how can I best identify and address these?'* Ensure that those in your inner circle feel psychologically safe enough to challenge your decisions and highlight them when it looks like motives have become mixed. (**Note**: you need to build that culture of psychological safety amongst those closest to you and within your team. It does not automatically appear with your role or develop overnight, but leading consistently with good character and building trust lays the foundation for a safe, challenging culture, which requires constant nurturing).

Is pride something you believe everyone else struggles with, but you are immune to or have mastered it years ago? If you do, that is pride talking! As part of being honest with ourselves, we need to spot and remove pride from our motives. Most times, we need others to help us spot it. Staying teachable also positions us to recognise it. Sadly, the relevant question to ask ourselves is rarely, *'Am I operating in pride somewhere?'* Personally, I have found it more realistic to ask myself, *'Where am I acting in pride?'* This perspective keeps my feet on the ground and is more effective in minimising pride growth.

> We naturally think of things that benefit us first.

Remember that none of us is better than anyone else, or worse. We may be stronger or more talented in a few areas compared to others, but they have strengths where we do not, so we are in no place to look down on anyone or think we are superior. Pride is really fuelled by insecurity. As mentioned earlier, the more we value and accept ourselves, cultivating contentment in our current state while moving towards who and where we want to be, the healthier our perspective becomes.

Think about it: The best inventions, discoveries, and achievements have ALL involved collaboration with others to larger or lesser extents, and ALL serve other people.

>> Think about it for a moment:

Are you proactive in identifying your blind spots?

What area of your life is too focused on you?

When was the last time you did a pride audit?

Stinginess

Do you ever feel better after spending time with stingy people? The only time I think we can come close is when we have a similar mindset, but even then, we judge ourselves differently from how we see others.

Stinginess is rooted in a fear of lack. It may result from a bad experience or having been taken advantage of. Both poor and wealthy people can be stingy, and it is not exclusively linked to money. We can be stingy with our time for others or with the level of self-care we demonstrate. The character, Scrooge, is a recognisable example of stinginess, but do not assume that stinginess is always this obvious or as extreme.

It is an outlook, an attitude, a perspective on life and what is valuable to us and others, which can be confronted and changed if desired. It may be justified by pride, thinking that we are better than someone and that they are where they are due to mistakes or poor decisions they have made. Or we may hold on to our resources, feeling that we have earned them.

The world of the stingy person gets smaller, not larger

There is nothing wrong with having things and enjoying them, provided we stay in control of them instead of them controlling us. It is for us to judge ourselves as to whether we have a stingy or generous outlook. Others may observe one particular action of ours (whether stingy or generous) and assume that this is our normal mode of operation when, in fact, it may not be. We know ourselves and the reasons why we do certain things. We may want to appear generous and, therefore, visibly donate to a charity. However, if we do not give with a generous motive from our hearts, we are operating in deception.

Release to receive

> We cannot accumulate more by withholding.

There is a subtle but powerful law woven into the fabric of our universe that requires an exchange or change for growth and expansion to occur. It is subtle because the return we get from exchanging, i.e., giving our time, finances, attention, releasing something, etc., is not always immediate—picture two farmers, both with a bag of seeds. One stores the seeds, and the other sows them in the right soil. One still possesses a bag of seeds, and the other does not. After a passage of time, the farmer who sowed his seed (given the right environmental conditions and level of associated activities) will gain a large return from what he sowed, which includes more seeds to sow again. The other farmer will still have a bag of seeds, which by now may have rotted. We cannot accumulate more by withholding.

The opposite of being stingy is not carelessly distributing our abilities or resources without thought or discernment as to where, when, or the measure that we invest and give of what we have control over.

Healthy self-leadership regularly checks our thoughts and motives regarding our giving or when we choose not to. Leaving a stingy thought or action unchecked can develop into a mindset that will propagate a habit of similar actions, restricting your life and leadership.

>>Think about it for a moment:

Have you identified an area where you are holding on to something you know should be given away?

Is there a relationship or an activity where you need to redirect time or attention towards or away from?

Is there an area where you are giving too much of something?

*"Doing what is most beneficial,
when you need to do it,
and…
choosing to be happy
about it!"*

CHAPTER SEVEN

Allies or Enemies – you decide!

Friend or foe to you? These elements affect the effectiveness of our self-leadership and are listed because they are neither just allies nor enemies by themselves (this is not the full list of elements). Their status is determined by how we use them. However, this does not mean they are neutral or passive. If they are not working FOR you and you are not using them intentionally, by default, they are working against you! (This theme is repeated several times for learning). These are not listed in a specific order, but I would place 'mindset' as something to assess first because of the influence it has on everything else.

Mindset

Mindset is a habitual way of thinking that sees from a particular perspective (influenced by your paradigm). *[See also Another paradigm?]*. In a simple form, a healthy mindset could be *[fill in the blank]*.

Mindset = '_____ is what I want/am called to do…and I am going to do it.'

Could it be as simple as this? In theory, yes, if we stay focused and not get seduced by distractions. But in reality, it takes a lot more work! As with our bodies, our minds were designed for regular activity and stimulation. Your mind is a powerhouse working constantly, but is it working for or against you? Imagine that your mind is like a firehose. With the force of water gushing through the hose, if the hose is not controlled, it will whip around in all directions and potentially cause damage and injury. Uncontrolled thoughts will whip our focus and emotions around in all directions, causing a lack of focus and confusion. We then lose effectiveness and increase the likelihood of hurting ourselves and others.

So, check in regularly with your thinking and recognise what type of thoughts you are giving space to in your mind. Lead your thoughts in the direction you want them to go. We do not have to accept every thought that enters our minds. Filter them out by asking yourself, *'Does this thinking empower me? 'Will these thoughts take me closer to where I want to go or take me further from it?'*

Build a tenacity in your thinking and refuse to get taken off track by random 'trains' of thoughts heading to destinations you do not want to visit.

The internal mirror

How we see ourselves determines our thinking, feelings, and actions. It leads to our results. If we allow a poor self-image to develop and remain within us, it will establish a mindset that accommodates any thought that does not empower us to become who we want to be and can be. Giving thinking space to these thoughts limits us and mars our self-worth, working against ourselves and unleashing an internal civil war! Do not disqualify yourself in your thinking from being successful, starting a business, relocating to a new city, or moving beyond your current 'normal'. What is normal now was once a stretch.

> Lead your thoughts in the direction you want them to go.

The empowering reality is that <u>we can choose what we think about</u>. This means we can change and build a healthy self-image and mindset. We can choose the type of thoughts we keep and the ones to discard. Dr Caroline Leaf writes, *'Whatever you think about the most will grow…like watering a plant'*.[24] We can focus our thinking with intentional, recurring thoughts to grow a healthy mindset. Fortifying your mind and cultivating a healthy thought life determine the level of success you will experience. This needs to be a lifestyle to really leverage the power of consistency, not a practice we participate in occasionally.

'The mind is a creature of habit. It thrives upon the dominating thoughts fed it.' – Napoleon Hill [25]

Important areas (also elaborated on in other sections) when it comes to developing a leadership mindset:

Self-belief	What does the inner voice tell you regularly? Is it creating the image of the future that you want? Belief determines behaviour, so check your habits and actions to identify the beliefs driving them.
Personal growth	Avoid settling for life under your current 'lid' of beliefs and expectations about yourself and your capabilities.
Clarity	Clarity is the precursor to focused energy. Why do you do what you currently do? Do your goals, habits, and actions align with where you actually want to go or who you want to become?
Focus	Focus maximises resources and minimises waste when aimed productively. The sharper you can stay focused, the more success you will experience. Did you ever try the experiment with a magnifying glass and a leaf where you focus sunlight on a specific part of the leaf? What was the outcome? The more concentrated the

	sunlight, the quicker it burns a hole in the leaf! How 'laser-focused' are you currently?
Repetition	Consistency compounds. Which habits and routines (those repetitive actions you do either consciously or unconsciously) currently serve the intentional cultivation of healthy thinking?
	Develop learned responses to things and events. Whenever I stub my toe or hit my knee on a chair (which happens more often than you would imagine!), I have learned to be thankful 'automatically'. I was not thankful that I felt discomfort, but thankful for the fact that I *could feel* discomfort. The more self-aware we are of our learned responses, the more we can decide if they are the most appropriate responses and not just bad habitual responses.
Resilience	We only really develop resilience during tough times! High emotional intelligence (EQ) enables us to think clearly and make objective decisions to develop resilience.
	There is great power in expectation and optimism. We arm ourselves well for life's challenges when we expect them to come. I am not advocating that we should always expect bad or tough things to happen. However, we must realise that we will encounter our 'fair share' of unexpected events, disappointments, tragedies, and opposition, times when we fail to reach our goal(s), and moments when we want to quit pursuing our dreams.
	Determine beforehand that you will navigate these times optimistically, looking for the positives, and that they will not 'take you out of the game' but will pass at some point. Just keep moving forward and growing. Adopt the stance that, despite the challenges and resistance, you would rather 'be in the game' than sit on the sidelines.

Here are some useful habits to implement to aid in developing a healthy mindset:

1. Keep a mental grip on your vision – hold it at the forefront of your thinking and let it grow. Give yourself time to think. Continue to picture it in your mind and let your imagination build it, wrapped in feel-good emotions.

2. Regular input from carefully selected people:

    i. Mentor(s) (who you may or may never meet).

    ii. A coach (who may be long-distance. Many clients I coach live in other nations).

    iii. Family or a close friend you can confide in who will support your vision.

3. Regular physical activity (find what works for you) and regular breaks. These help to clear our minds so that we can refocus. Include at times, a break from technology.

4. Do something you are passionate about regularly (avoid getting too busy and making excuses to squeeze this out).

5. Speak out positive affirmations about yourself and your future. We believe what we hear ourselves say more than anyone else, whether good or bad.

6. Do not hold grudges - holding grudges is toxic!! (Here is a perspective shift: what if our 'enemies' are just people with a story we do not yet understand?). Grudges are distractions. Whenever we are reminded of the scenario or see the person involved, the negative emotions arise again and change our mood. Do not let them control you; control them by letting them go.

7. Practise being thankful for what you have AND what you do not have.

> >> Think about it for a moment:
>
> Pause and think about what you have been thinking about already today. What thoughts have empowered you to focus, feel positive, and empower others?
>
> What thoughts have drained you of energy and happiness and made you feel limited?
>
> What are some of your dominant, recurring thoughts?
>
> Do you have a clear vision or image that pulls you forward and influences your actions?
>
> Are you keeping the main thing a priority in your mind?

Choice

So much in life—how we live, what we spend time on, and who we spend time with, is determined by our choices. Some are out of our control, but good self-leadership focuses on what we can control. Choices are controlling every moment of our lives. We should regularly examine whether we are making choices that contribute to positive things or choosing things to our detriment. Are our choices increasing or reducing stress in our lives and others? (Their outcome may not be evident immediately).

Are you setting the pace of your life by the choices you make, or is someone or something else determining this?

Are you choosing to do things that bring happiness and contentment, or have you surrendered these aspects to be determined by the outcome of others' choices?

Are your current choices vitiating your leadership?

Everything we do, even to the smallest degree, either moves us towards where we want to go or takes us away from it

Choices are chisels

We can use choices to design and produce the life we desire. When no moral implication is involved, a choice is based more on preference or practicality. There are no 'wrong' answers as such, just different outcomes, which are likely to contain a mix of pros and cons. Choices are the chisels that sculpt our lives. A sculptor sees more than just the block of wood or the piece of stone or clay in front of them. They have an image in their minds of what the block will become. They change the external image of what is before them to represent their internal image. That image informs and directs how they choose to use the chisel, which parts are cut off, and which are shaped in a certain way. We all have a picture of our lives, where we would like to be, and who we would like to become. If we are bold enough, we plan and choose to pursue this. Or do we just keep it as a dream, someplace we escape to in our imagination when reality is uncomfortable? Do you really believe you can get there, or are you distracted by what you can see externally and allowing that to determine how or what you choose?

Choices produce fruit, so examine what they are producing, and if it is not what you want, make changes where possible. But consider that not every choice we make brings an immediate result. There is an element of faith in many of our decisions. We believe it is the right thing to do even though, at the time, it may not feel like it or there is no immediate evidence to back this up. Standing on your conviction and choice, regardless of what circumstances may be saying, is a great quality of self-leadership, provided we remain flexible enough to make appropriate changes if this requirement becomes evident. You have chisels; how will you use them?

Circumstances are the result of choices

You may be thinking that *circumstances* are controlling your life. Have you had a traumatic experience that has left an indelible mark on your soul? Something happened that you did not choose, were not responsible for, or was unjust and wrong, but you were powerless to stop? This was the result of someone else's choice(s). Their choice and behaviour shaped a part of your life that did not align with your inner image or dream for the future. You do not have to allow that experience to restrict and control you, harming and redefining the image inside. There are steps you can take and professionals you can collaborate with to walk through the pain, find healing, and move on to a brighter future. Good self-leadership controls how we respond and frame (or reframe) these events. Are you going to navigate a tough challenge with a positive outcome, making good choices, deciding to grow, and choosing to find some good within it? Or will you live as a victim wounded by other people's chisels?

Life is in motion, are you?

Life is constantly in motion. Where we choose to step determines our direction and leads us to a certain destination. Since the introduction of fitness trackers and smart apps, there has been a lot of emphasis on how many steps we track during a day. This can fuel an increase in exercise by raising our awareness of how much movement we participate in over a period of time. We then decide if the measure of effort and exertion recorded is acceptable to us, whether as part of a stringent exercise routine or as a more leisurely analysis of activity and general health, and then respond accordingly. So, whatever number of steps you achieve, are they taking you where you want to go? Are you making your steps count, or are you just counting steps?

There are three types of steps we choose to take:

1. **Steps that take us towards where we want to go** – taking steps to achieve defined goals, including making adjustments as things change. It ensures we are always moving in the right direction.

2. Steps that maintain our current lifestyle – these are more like treading water. They are the essentials we need to do to stay as we are, nothing more. They can be useful in a limited capacity, as they enable us to resist the natural trend of regression from inactivity. Still, their purpose is more to maintain rather than move forward.
3. Steps that cause us to regress and go backwards – when we lose focus or give up hope in response to failure or adverse circumstances, we can get distracted and pulled off course. This results in us taking steps that start to move us away from our ideal destination. Or it may be that we neglect self-care, and exhaustion can blur our focus and ability to make wise decisions.

> Are you making your steps count, or are you just counting steps?

Every step takes you somewhere...

>>Think about it for a moment:

Are you working towards making your inner picture a reality with defined goals and activities?

Can you identify a choice hindering you from moving in this direction?

How productive are your current steps regarding the direction you want to go?

Perspective

Having a realistic perspective when approaching anything sets us up better for success. Great leaders understand that they are responsible for setting the vision for the way ahead, making tough decisions when necessary, and seeing things before others see them to prevent or mitigate issues. We can become too close to things happening in the moment, which can hinder our perspective. We must mentally lift ourselves out of the immediate to view things from a bigger perspective regularly. So often, things in the 'now' moments demand our attention and decisions. I learnt this valuable lesson the hard way. While leading a service delivery team at a conference during a particularly busy period, as I like to be 'hands-on' with activities and help the team, I got involved with the task at hand. It was good and useful, and it encouraged the team. But I stayed in this activity too long. Another part of the process I was responsible for was having an issue I was unaware of because my focus was too concentrated on the immediate need we were addressing.

I like the picture of mentally getting into a helicopter to rise above immediate things demanding your attention, to lift your gaze above these and expand your view to see better how things interact on a broader scale. This can enable you to solve problems more efficiently and quicker, stop issues from growing and multiplying, as well as inform you of how and when best to reallocate resources.

Then, when necessary, take this example a step further. Beyond the 'helicopter' view is the 'satellite' view. This provides a more expansive view and a 'global' perspective, not just about how things you lead interact, but how your efforts and influence affect the wider world outside your operating environment, current clients, etc., and your level of influence on the planet!

The challenge, therefore, is to navigate between these views appropriately and spend the right amount of time on each perspective, informing immediate decisions and future planning. It is highly likely that most of the people you lead, unless trained differently, will never think about seeing things from a helicopter or satellite view, but you can change this.

Having a bad day?

Do you see life generally as bad but with some good moments or good but with some challenges? It comes back to a 'glass half full/half empty' perspective, OR just thankful that you have a glass!

I really believe that **'those who see good in everything will never be defeated!'** I intentionally decided years ago that I would never again have a 'bad day'. Now, I recognised that there would be *moments* I would consider 'bad' and negative, but I determined that I would never write off a day or excuse my actions and attitude by saying, *"I'm just having a bad day"*. This perspective enables me to minimise the negative effect a scenario may have while not denying its existence or how I need to respond. It may be that the negative fall-out spans longer than 24 hours, BUT that does not mean every part of each day has to be negative. I have worked with colleagues who, when they see that it is raining, say, *'It's a miserable day'*, to which I think, and sometimes reply, *'No, it's just rain. I'm thankful we are waterproof!'*

There is scientific proof that disturbed sleep affects our performance.[26] Think about the last time you had a disturbed night. Although you may have felt a bit 'under par', how much did your perspective about the missed sleep affect your thinking and performance throughout that day? Was it just a moment, and you 'shook it off', or did you carry it around as the excuse for everything that went less than ideal? Keep it as a momentary event in your perspective to minimise the power it has to influence more time than it should. Time moves one way; it is what it *was*, so move on.

A dog's life

> A next-door neighbour owns several dogs. Most of the time, they are quiet, but when the last person in the house leaves each day, the smallest dog starts barking for around 30 minutes every day! I think it then tires because it goes quiet until the following day when the last person leaves again. When the dog barks, the owner does not suddenly return home. They return when they are ready,

> REGARDLESS of whether the dog barks or not. As I thought about this, I realised that we could behave similarly. When things are not going as we would like, do we just bark about it, OR do we accept what we cannot control, change our perspective, and look to make the best of where we are and what we can control?

At any moment, we have 'a' perspective, just *one* viewpoint of situations that will differ from others. Embrace the perspective of appreciating everyone. I believe there are some absolutes that the universe operates by, but we need to allow others to have their perspective too and be open to adopting theirs if it is appropriate. Have you ever been surprised and frustrated when something you believe as universally true and beneficial to everyone is not accepted by other people? (e.g., that it is always better to love others than hate them). Allow other people to have their perspective. Also, work with what you can, find common ground where possible, and agree to disagree where differences persist. As long as we remain agile, teachable, and willing to embrace new ideas, we position ourselves for ongoing growth. Hence, we must avoid bigotry without compromising our core values, realising that we do not have all the answers and that what seems right for one person may not be right for another.

> Time moves one way…

No 'Plan B' on purpose

I always live in 'Plan A'. Impressed? Let me explain more. This was a decision I made a long time ago to never live believing I am living second best in 'Plan B' when my ideal life exists in 'Plan A'. This perspective shift can make all the difference in our hope, expectation, and belief in what is possible. Now, to clarify, I regularly need to readjust 'Plan A' with different versions! But always positioning my perspective from 'Plan A', regardless of how many variations I need to make, keeps me living in my best potential. This is not trying to deceive myself, but it is a conscious choice that positively influences my energy, beliefs, and results.

Another paradigm?

Do you need a paradigm shift? Our paradigm is a collection of beliefs operating from our subconscious mind that produces behaviour patterns. It is the frame of reference we use that influences and shapes our perception. Stephen Covey defines a paradigm as *'...the way we 'see' the world – not in terms of our visual sense of sight, but in terms of perceiving, understanding, interpreting.'*[27] Paradigms are both personal and public. This book is written from my current personal paradigm, but it will become public. Some will agree with it, while others will not. On the flip side, you are reading this from your current personal paradigm. Another example of a public paradigm on a national scale would be a country's culture.

Paradigms are formed through dramatic or long-term experiences and repetition. If we experience an abusive situation, when we find ourselves, even years later, in a situation that has some similarities, we can assume or expect the same things to happen because our paradigm, shaped by previous abuse, brings recollection, interprets this scenario, and influences our thinking and behaviours accordingly. The well-known phrase 'hurt people hurt people' sums this up. While hurt people may not intentionally be trying to hurt others, acting out of that hurt is likely to be defensive, critical, etc., and fuelled by the instinct for self-preservation and protection.

Can you see the power and profitability of operating from a positive paradigm? Drawing from a core belief based on positive hope, we can view every scenario as an opportunity to grow, prosper, and assist others. Having a positive perspective as we enter and work through challenges and are confronted by the pain and wickedness in our world, we can take the 'higher ground'. We become part of the solution instead of contributing to the problem. I believe good will always prevail in the end because love is way more powerful than hate.

What about you?

Have you considered whether others would rate your self-leadership and see it as selfless as you would? Often, we judge others by their actions, but we judge ourselves by our intentions. We can be positively (and unconsciously) biased and justify what we do, or if we have low self-esteem, we are more inclined to be overly critical of ourselves. Are there one or two people you know well, who understand self-leadership and whose perspective you can trust? Have a conversation with them. As part of evaluating where you are and what you need to change, think about this:

If you were not you, would you follow you?

Developing a healthy self-belief and perspective of yourself has multiple benefits. For a start, you will enjoy your own company more. However, having healthy self-belief positively influences our perspective, which means we operate at a level where tackling and overcoming challenges is easier.

>>Think about it for a moment:

Do you regularly navigate between the helicopter and satellite views when required?

How tolerant are you towards others with a different perspective?

How well do you handle the differences?

Would you be willing to follow you? *[Can you explain why?]*

Focus

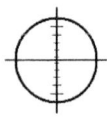

Can you remember what it is like to look at an old photo that was taken out of focus? It is blurry and difficult to identify details. Now, unless the intention was to compliment the subject by applying a soft focus, the photo is less than ideal and not as excellent as it could have been.

What we focus on expands, so this will either benefit or harm our self-leadership. Where your attention goes, your energy flows. We have a limited amount of time and energy each day. While I am not advocating constraining ourselves with too much intensity by locking down every moment with a specific activity, there are huge benefits in knowing what you want or need to do, and channelling your attention and resources towards these.

There is a universal truth that I have experienced first-hand: 'Work expands to fill the time'. I have occasionally realised that if I have an hour to do a 30-minute activity, unless I am intentionally focused, I can spend the full hour on it, 'perfecting' it. Some of that time could have been better spent elsewhere, but because I could spend an hour on it, I did. Spending longer on a task than is actually necessary brings diminishing returns to our time. How many moments or work hours have been underutilised by a lack of focus?

Catch the lightning!

Awareness and focus work together.

> While on holiday in the south of France, I had the amazing experience of watching a storm in the distance while I sat on the beach. As we looked across the bay, the storm had reached the mainland opposite. There was forked lightning clearly visible across the expanse of the night sky in front of us. It was amazing and unforgettable!

Have you ever tried to catch a glimpse of forked lightning? If your view is more restricted than mine was, you can gaze into the sky with a certain awareness of the area it may strike. However, when you happen to place your focus exactly where the lightning bolt appears, you can clearly see the fork strike, if only for a brief moment. The flip side of this is that when you are looking at something without being aware of it, you see it but do not really see or register it consciously. It does not reach your conscious awareness.

More of less

As a keen reader, I can easily find myself reading five books at a time. Do you read multiple books at once? Now, there can be benefits to doing this sometimes, particularly if each book covers a different subject matter that you are researching or if you are doing more of a deep dive into one specific topic. But on other occasions, there is more benefit in just choosing one book to focus our reading time on. We can then absorb from it the truth that will equip and guide us to where we are at that point. I really believe that the measure of thought and study we give to the truth that we hear determines the level of understanding and insight we receive from it. Truth is pregnant with multiple layers of insight, which we can often skip over at surface level and miss the depths completely. This is when we need more of less. More time and attention on fewer things.

How much time do you spend thinking about what you listen to? You could hear this question in multiple ways. For example, how specific and focused am I about making sure I listen to the things that will enable me to grow and develop in the areas that I want to? [See also *Inputs...*]. Or, how much time do I spend reflecting on the things that I actually listen to? Let us focus on this second perspective.

> The measure of thought and study we give to the truth that we hear determines the level of understanding and insight we receive from it.

We are in a very privileged place in history when you look at the level of accessibility we have to a diverse range of information. This can be really beneficial, provided we do not become gluttonous in our approach to consuming it. It is easy to jump from one podcast episode to another, attend a live virtual event, catch a webinar recording, or participate in multiple conferences. And these can all be useful and healthy if kept in balance. But are we really assimilating and allowing what we hear to take root in our thinking and memory with the level of focus that will benefit us? Are we changed by what we hear? Do we pause and reflect on it, looking for ways to apply what we are learning so it improves our thinking, behaviours and performance? Or do we just move on to the next item of input? *[See also Reflection]*. Taking time to reflect enables us to consolidate our learning. Learning is for growth so that we can do better. Do not expect that more learning will automatically equal more growth (if you do not retain it or apply it). Similarly, do not hide within learning and learn for the sake of it. Always look to act on what you are learning.

Two-stage examples

Consumption vs absorption - **When we eat a meal, our body starts to absorb and process the nutrients from the food and liquid we have consumed. It identifies and uses what it needs to stay healthy, grow, and develop, then discards the fibre and other parts it does not need. This process takes time. If we just consumed a meal that went straight through our bodies and bypassed the absorption process, we would not only miss out on the benefits of the nutrients we ate but also feel less satisfied. We will feel hungry again a lot sooner. When it comes to learning, developing our intellect, changing our mindsets, and challenging how or why we currently think about things, we need to be consciously and actively involved in that process. Giving ourselves time to reflect curiously helps us digest what we have consumed. If we try to eat too much food at once, we will feel overwhelmed and uncomfortable. It will stress the whole digestion process.**

Downloading AND installing - **Most apps require regular updates to fix bugs, provide enhancements, improve the user experience, or add new features. This is usually a two-step process. First, the device running the app must download the update, and second, the update needs to be installed. There has to be a process of installing the upgrade into the app so that it becomes part of the operating system. If we continue using the app after the update** has been downloaded but not installed, we will not benefit from the bug fixes or new features. We have the potential, but we will operate at the same level as before. We need to allow it to install, assimilate, and become part of our new operating system so that we can then function at that higher level. Both steps must be performed before we can benefit from the changes.

Focus your focus

To determine what it is you need to prioritise and focus your focus on, ask yourself:

'How can I best spend this time?'
'Will doing _____ contribute to or help me realise what I want to achieve?'
'How important really is it if _____ does not happen?'
'What is the knock-on effect if _____ does not happen?'
'Am I determining this as a priority, or is someone else?'

Once you have identified areas to focus on, you can utilise the 'Brain Warm-up' tool devised by Risa Williams in *The Ultimate Time Management Toolkit*.[28] It is a simple tool that helps prime your brain to engage in a focused activity better. Since reading her book, I have adopted this and actually used it before I sat down to write more of this book! For me, a 5-minute burst of doing a Sudoku puzzle gets me sharp. I keep the setting on the 'Easy' level and attempt to complete it in 5 minutes or less. Sometimes, I am successful. But a note of caution if you decide to adopt something similar. After achieving a good average of successfully completing these in less than 5 minutes, I ventured to the 'Medium' level until, after a few attempts, I realised that I had started to focus too much brain energy on the puzzle instead of keeping this as a warm-up exercise to prime me for the 'main event'!

> \>\> Think about it for a moment:
>
> Are you clear about where your main focus is right now?
>
> Can you identify an area where your focus needs to shift to something different?

> Are you spending the right time on tasks proportionate to their importance or requirements?
>
> If you could make one adjustment right now to give you the best return on your focus, what would it be?

Failure

Failure can stop you in your tracks, rob you of self-esteem, and in extreme cases, cause you to give up all hope. When you fail (and if we are honest, we all do), do you wallow in disappointment, or do you realise that we usually 'fail our way to success'? Have you yet to embrace the reality that:

- a) you have failed (because you refuse to admit it)?
- b) you will fail again at some point in the future (probably multiple times)?
- c) sometimes, when things go wrong, it is your fault (or do you try to blame someone else)?

If you have not yet accepted these, you will constantly struggle.

There is naturally a negative emotion connected to failure because, except in rare cases,* we never set out to fail! But good self-leadership helps us work past this emotion and make it positive by reframing the experience and encouraging ourselves that we are expanding our experiences by trying something new.

In weight training, taking muscles to failure demonstrates that you have maxed out your rep potential at that point – the muscle can no longer contract concentrically, which, it is reported, can create more muscle stimulation, potentially boosting improvements to muscle strength once recovered.

Failing does not mean you are a failure!

Permission to fail

You have my permission to fail. You do not *need* my permission, but you have it anyway. Go for it. Whatever the dream you hold inside, if it will not harm anyone else, you have my permission to proceed. How will you know unless you attempt to make it happen? You may surprise yourself.

It is a peculiar thought, is it not, that we often do not start or continue with something because we are waiting for someone else to grant us permission? And this may not be anyone specific! We feel comfort when someone communicates their support for us, even if we do not achieve what we expected or imagined or if the achievement takes a different form. But taking this stance puts our power under someone else's control.

Have you given yourself permission to fail? Have you allowed yourself that grace to mess up and still appreciate who you are, see yourself as valuable, and pursue a different route or approach?

Making failure work for us

From every failing scenario, we would ideally learn more about:

- Ourselves – how we respond, communicate, and process the outcome.
- Others involved – recognise support or hindrances, etc.
- Our environment/the circumstance – contributing factors to failure.
- Our approach – what we could do differently.

At the very least, when we learn more about ourselves, including the reasons behind our actions, the feelings driving those actions, and the thoughts behind those feelings, we grow and increase our self-awareness, thereby improving our understanding.

Remember that no one is born knowing things (excluding instincts). The knowledge and understanding we each have now have been developed over time through what we have heard and experienced.

Some positives about failure:

1. When we examine why we failed, what we omitted that would have avoided failure, did we overdo something, etc.? It means we discover changes to make in ourselves or externally.

2. Failure shows that we are trying something new, stepping out of our comfort zone, leaving the safe, often mediocre, realm to experiment, bring about change, and create something from our minds into reality. Great self-leadership MUST involve regularly leaving and expanding our comfort zone. We cannot get to a higher level of operation or living just by continuing to do the same things that have gotten us to where we are now. We have to stretch.

3. You have found a way that does not work.

Now, the smart approach is to gather the right people and resources and collate enough information to make informed decisions. You should also be able to manage or mitigate risks wherever possible before taking any steps, investing, starting conversations, or approaching situations. But even when we do this due diligence, we cannot guarantee that we have eradicated the failure option. We do not see what we do not see.

> Great self-leadership MUST involve regularly leaving and expanding our comfort zone.

>> Think about it for a moment:

What failure (if any) are you struggling to move on from?

What learning can you gain from that experience?

How would you do things differently now?

What is that experience stopping you from doing now?

Fear

Fear can work for us, although it is usually found as the culprit for inactivity or underperformance, limiting our exploration of ourselves and the world around us and resulting in mediocre living. It can be the thief that steals opportunity and new experiences. There are benefits to living in a 'steady' state, where we feel balanced, in control, knowing what will happen, and free to make decisions. But constantly operating in this state without expanding ourselves becomes counterproductive, breeding stagnation and regression.

> Fear is a tester of how much we really want something.

Often, the feeling of fear occurs when this steady state is challenged, and it is time to grow.

Circumstances change, and we can feel forced into the unknown or we become aware of a 'knowing' inside of us, (that gut feeling which, in my experience, we should respond to more often than not instead of suppressing it). This feeling also prompts us to do something we would find uncomfortable or that involves risk of failure, embarrassment, or loss. Fear is a tester of how much we really want something. Why, when we can live differently, would we allow fear to hinder us?

As with other elements, perspective can help us see things clearer, as the extent of what we think we are afraid of is at least partly imaginary. Except where there is immediate danger, the feeling of fear, which emanates from our thinking, can be the prompt for us to realise that we have the opportunity to stretch ourselves, explore the unknown, and take steps outside of our comfort zone. This allows us to grow, expand our skills and understanding, and in turn, assist in the development of others. As we recognise this, the more we control our imagination, the better we lead ourselves.

When we separate anxious feelings regarding the issue and check in with ourselves, realising that being on the other side of it, with accompanying results, would be beneficial, liberating, and empowering, this perspective reduces fear. Realising these benefits then becomes a more motivating force than the desire to 'stay safe'.

Turn on the light

Fear often lurks in the dark areas of the unknown; therefore, by increasing our understanding of the actual reality and reminding ourselves of what we are capable of (based on past experiences and successes), we increase the light of our awareness and the fear usually shrinks. Our perspective shifts. Think about a time when you faced a fear and survived, when you 'called its bluff'. How good did that feel? How small did the fear actually look afterwards?

Once you are aware that you feel fear or anxiety about taking action, follow these steps:

1. Note down what makes you afraid – having a difficult conversation, presenting results, etc.
2. Identify why this feels scary. Specific attributes and contributors. Talking this through with someone else often makes the fear smaller.
3. Balance this by asking, *'What is the worst that could happen, really?'*
4. Think through the positive outcome of completing or achieving the action—results, feelings, benefits, etc. Where do you want to go? Who do you want to become? Embrace this version of you. See yourself as bigger and more successful than you feel now.
5. What things can you do beforehand, or what support or resources can you utilise to make the scenario more pleasant? What actions can you take to increase the likelihood of success and reduce anxiety?
6. Evaluate:
    a. Does this fear outweigh your desire?
    b. Is it really more powerful than your potential?

> >> Think about it for a moment:
>
> What area of your life has been stalled by fear?
>
> How can you approach this differently?
>
> What will it feel like to be on the other side of it?
>
> What opportunities will this open up?

Humour

There are many instances when life is just plain funny! And when we do not take ourselves too seriously, we can see the funny side in our behaviour and thoughts too (as well as those of others!). In addition, whether we take a more optimistic stance in life or not, we ALL can find humour in everyday situations and share something amusing with others. There are great health benefits to laughter and having fun. When experienced correctly, e.g., it discharges nervous energy, relaxes the mind and body by releasing endorphins, and reduces stress by lowering cortisol levels.[29] Have you noticed how we are attracted to funny people and tend to remember more things that make us laugh?

This brings me to why this is listed here and not just as an ally. Humour is best used with respect when we laugh *with* others, not *at* others. Ensure that the humour is inclusive and has the right motive when having fun. Does the root of your humour actually put others down? Great leadership nurtures a culture that empowers others to reach new levels of growth, performance, and self-belief, thereby increasing competence and confidence. Insecure leaders look to put others down to elevate themselves.

> Laugh *with* others, not *at* others.

Some consider sarcasm humour, but it is often used to cloak mockery and derision. If used satirically, sarcasm can amusingly reveal the folly of an action, etc.

Can you laugh at yourself in a healthy way? If not, you will struggle to keep humour as an ally. A healthy self-leadership perspective centralises us on the road of life. It keeps us from either being in the ditch on one side where we are too rigid, intense, serious, and cannot laugh at our mistakes. Or falling into the ditch on the other side that sees everything as a joke, diminishing the importance of maturing and addressing serious issues and undermining trustworthiness with responsibility.

When having fun, we are more relaxed and in a better state to lead others

Humour can be a powerful tool to lead people out of negativity and unproductive emotions, but pick your moment and be sensitive to their feelings. It can remind us that life is not as serious as we sometimes make it out to be. Being able to laugh effectively during tense situations can also contribute to building self-esteem and releasing more creativity because it increases positivity in our mood, which can attract hope (even in the most adverse situations).

Leaders contribute to setting and governing the team atmosphere, so to avoid stress becoming unbalanced in your team, ensure there is:

- a healthy blend of respect for others,
- a realisation of the importance of discipline and focused effort, AND
- fun thrown into the mix of all your endeavours.

This starts with us internally. Healthy humour makes the environment a better place to be and is a strong ally when you experience life at its most absurd.

> **>> Think about it for a moment:**
>
> Check in with yourself to ensure that the motive driving your humour is selfless.
>
> Can you discern between times when you have laughed *with* others and laughed *at* them?
>
> Do you need to apologise first to be able to build a healthier, more humorous environment?
>
> Where can you bring more positive humour to those in your world?

Success

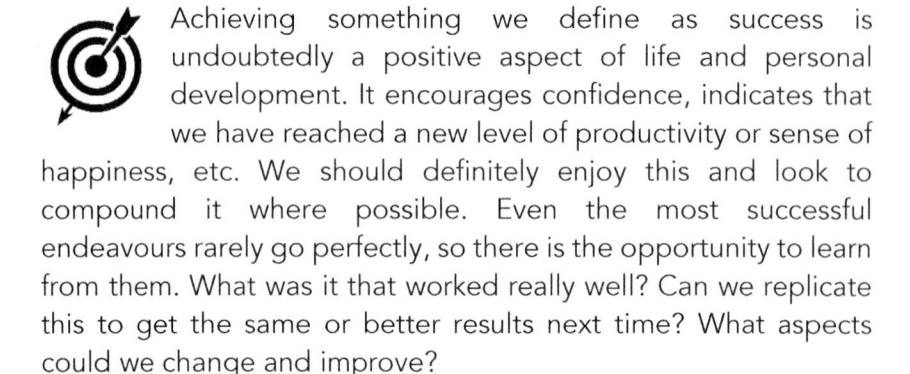

Achieving something we define as success is undoubtedly a positive aspect of life and personal development. It encourages confidence, indicates that we have reached a new level of productivity or sense of happiness, etc. We should definitely enjoy this and look to compound it where possible. Even the most successful endeavours rarely go perfectly, so there is the opportunity to learn from them. What was it that worked really well? Can we replicate this to get the same or better results next time? What aspects could we change and improve?

Even better next time?

> For many years, I led service teams within part of the operations element at large conferences for a not-for-profit. There was a healthy leadership culture, and as part of a team of leaders in different areas, we sought feedback from each other and those on our teams after each event. This would feed into the overall team review to determine how to improve the next event.
>
> This is a great habit to adopt because it is easy to operate from your view of things and go from activity to activity,

particularly within a full schedule, but not actually make time to allow for improvements. It also shows that you value individual input and are open to continual learning and flexibility. The best way to do something may well be within a team member, just waiting to surface and be released. But ensure that you do more than just collect feedback and complete it as an exercise. To encourage future input, it is imperative that lessons learnt are followed by instigating aligned changes, which are communicated to relevant parties.

During times of doubt or uncertainty, remind yourself of past successes. Let them inspire you. They can really boost and strengthen your confidence and focus, which can be channelled effectively. The more positive a state we keep ourselves in and operate from, the easier it will be to recognise the best way forward, stay resilient, and behave wisely. But do not define who you are by your success. Instead, define your success based on who you are.

Success can change identity and become an enemy to us when we allow our response to it to become unbalanced. While celebrating, we should mix it with humility. Acknowledge that others contributed to this happening, either directly or because of something someone said or did that influenced us earlier in life.

> Do not define who you are by your success; define your success by who you are.

This aids us from allowing pride and self-importance to rise above healthy levels. Alternatively, we can assume we know it all and stop listening to the best approach for the same scenario next time, or become closed to our intuition, leading to a lack of flexibility in our approach and development.

Another aspect of imbalance is when we give ourselves a disproportionate level of permission to ease up. We take our foot off the accelerator and start coasting along in life. Churchill said, *'Success is not final...'* [30] Now, there is nothing wrong with taking a break, particularly after intense or energetic effort, but as rest should be a regular habit, woven amongst good activity, our growth continues daily. So, enjoy success with the right measure, and then move on to continue the momentum.

>> Think about it for a moment:

Currently, how do you respond to success? Do you allow yourself to celebrate and enjoy it (including others who were involved)?

Think about your last success:

What elements made it successful?

What could you improve to achieve even more success?

What could you change or adapt to maximise resources and enhance efficiency?

The cost

There is a cost to successful self-leadership, but if you are yet to discover this, anything worth having costs us something to obtain and keep. The cost required is actually more of an ally because it forces you to evaluate if it is something you really value. If not, you will decide not to pay it. If you **DO** value it, but for one reason or another, procrastinate paying it, you will live at a lower level than you could, suppressing that desire and excusing your dream as some fantasy or something you will get to

> If self-leadership was easy, everyone would be a great leader.

'one day'. The cost, in varying forms, is ongoing and looks different at different times but will be a blend of elements, including:

- Sacrifice – is not a word we like to hear because it has the connotation of loss. Maybe if we reframed it, we would embrace sacrifice more often. It is actually linked to exchanging, where you offer something of value either to receive something of greater value or to support and contribute to a greater cause. We may not always see the direct benefit resulting from our sacrifice. At times, we must be willing to miss an event, a game, have a shorter rest period, etc., SO THAT we can _____ *[fill in the blank]* instead.

Keeping the bigger picture in mind when confronting the need to sacrifice provides a better opportunity for us to navigate this better. John Maxwell teaches that sacrifice is linked to two laws of development for Leadership & Personal Growth:

'The Law of Trade-offs – you have to give up to grow up' [31]

'The Law of Sacrifice – a leader must give up to go up'. [32]

Most things, if you disconnect the current emotion from them, seem less important a day or month later. However, at the time, if you just focus on the present moment, they can seem a lot more important than they actually are. When faced with sacrifice, imagine yourself one week or one year from now, looking back to the current. What do you think would have been the best decision to make now?

> *(**NOTE**: Do not use 'sacrifice' as an excuse for bad planning and then having to miss a key life event, like a child's first performance, time with your spouse on their birthday, etc. Remember to filter the decision through your values).*

- Money – this can be a real tester. Will you invest in the training, coaching, mentoring, and resources required to continually release more of your potential? (I do not mean constantly purchasing resources that you will never use or act on. Determine that you will not be part of the large majority that starts a book but never gets past the first chapter!). If you desire to grow but are unwilling to spend money on courses or seminars, your growth will be limited to what is offered 'free'. While some free resources can have a lot of value, you will inevitably have to part with money to grow deeper! If you view the money you invest as going into your future to improve it, it can make the decision easier.

In addition, you are actually leveraging the benefits of years of learning, experience, and lessons learned from experts specialising in a specific area(s) who provide growth resources and services. What took them 20 years to discover and refine is consolidated into courses, a programme, and so on. As a result, you can participate in the wealth of experience over a much shorter period of time. Growth does take time, BUT you can fast-track some of this by learning from experts and avoiding some of the pitfalls they experienced. You do not need to reinvent the wheel. Rather, think of how better, stronger, and sharper you will become by utilising the resources and services that you are investing in. But remember, investing money in resources for growth is only part of the equation. You then need to engage with them and take corresponding actions. I realised years ago that the easiest part of the process is purchasing a book, but that is only the start!

- Popularity – we have an intrinsic need to be connected to others and accepted by them. That is part of being human. The danger can be when we are challenged to stand by our convictions and make decisions that differ from their viewpoints or preferences, knowing that we will likely become less popular with them. If they disapprove, we may lose their support, friendship, and so on. Every situation needs to be judged based on the specific circumstances. Generally, there are times when communicating differences and why certain decisions were made provides healthy conflict. This allows people to discuss, evaluate, and, where necessary, agree to disagree. (They will usually respect you more for standing your ground). However, when this is not possible, great self-leadership guides us to stand firm regardless of the consequences and costs. If we compromise our values just to remain popular, we allow popularity and peer pressure to manipulate us, and we give our power to someone else.

- Comfort – if self-leadership was easy, everyone would be a great leader! To lead well, you must regularly make 'tough', uncomfortable decisions. Sometimes, the discomfort is not yours but for those you lead who do not, at this point, share the same opinion or perspective about the way forward. In these scenarios, you need to take extra steps and communicate or listen more to understand their concerns and, where possible, alleviate them.

- Short-term good feelings – we have all no doubt experienced moments when we would really like to lounge on the sofa and escape the current pressure by watching a movie, etc., but know that it is just not the best time to do so. We know that we have to take responsibility for something and focus on that instead. Scheduling a specific time to relax while sacrificing these feelings in the moment helps to balance the discomfort with hope.

Identify (and celebrate) an area where you have recently sacrificed something good for the sake of something great.

>>Think about it for a moment:

Is there an area where you could give something up now to advance quicker or more effectively on your growth journey?

Looking at the current level of finance that you invest in your growth, is this appropriate for the future you are building?

Is the pressure to conform hindering you from making effective decisions?

Time

Leading yourself well includes doing things when they need to get done, not necessarily when you want to, or feel like doing them, or when it is the most convenient. It will require making time available to focus on what you need to do, so something else will have to be paused, rescheduled, or missed to make this possible. Most of us underestimate how long it will take to complete tasks excellently. Often, we assign the length of time we would like the task to take, which does not always agree with reality. Also, when we experience high levels of stress, our perception of time shrinks.[33] So, where possible, avoid planning during these times.

Will you cut corners, reschedule, or sacrifice other activities less important, and give that endeavour the time and focus it needs?

Time provides a great structure for us to plan, schedule, and measure our lives. It can bring focus and urgency when needed. But now and again, I would encourage you to set aside a day without specific time demands to just be you. Reconnect with who you are and where you are in life. Use it as a time to check in with your dreams and your heart's desire. Allow yourself to imagine what that really feels like, and be open to inspiration from your intuition.

Even on holidays, we can adopt a similar schedule where we are controlled by time windows to visit somewhere while it is open or catch a boat trip. It is beneficial to periodically step out of time-bound routines and shift our perspective, particularly if attempting to achieve multiple deadlines creates pressure and unhealthy stress levels. When you start to feel that everything and everyone is pulling on you for input and time, this is a clear sign that things are out of balance and you are heading towards getting overwhelmed. Avoid getting to this point by 'stepping out of time', so to speak. Make time work for you. Remember:

Only prisoners serve time; time should serve us

Encouraging you to value your time is easy for me to write about, as this has been a passion of mine for a long time. You have probably heard it said that time is the most valuable resource we have that we cannot increase. Regardless of our levels of wealth or intelligence, no one can have days that exceed 24 hours. Remember that we can never get a moment back, and when we utilise moments well, it makes our future brighter.

A date with destiny

Every day has a destiny, but none has a duplicate. Each day has potential and boundaries beyond just sunrise and sunset. Within these boundaries, most of us have a lot of freedom in how we use the time given to us. But it is also important to be mindful that regardless of how we spend our day(s), we also have some limitations. There are some things that, no matter how much you try, will not happen on a specific day. For instance, you want to make an appointment, but none are available. Maybe you want to purchase something, but it is out of stock, and no other supplier has it either! It may be that the following day has the capacity for this endeavour, or maybe not. It could be that you are waiting on someone for something before you can complete a task.

Realising each day has a destiny removes some of the pressure to get certain 'stuff' done. I am definitely a proponent of planning and making the most out of life. It would be unwise to stand at the start of each day and just wait for something to happen unless you have intentionally cleared your schedule to rest and just 'flow'. We are initiators; that is part of our inherent nature (whether we

> There are some things that, no matter how much you try, will not happen on a specific day.

choose to accept it or not), and more so as you develop your leadership skills. But do not try to force things. Life is fluid. There is a natural flow to it, and while there are times when we need to overcome the resistance of circumstances (or from other people) or how we feel, discerning the flow makes the day more successful. Striving is counterproductive. Use your intuition to gauge what the day should hold for you, or at least, what is best to do in the moment you are in. What is your 'gut' saying? If this is unclear, start an activity and see if it 'feels right' to continue (if you have the option). Or provide support for someone else's focus, if appropriate.

From experience, although rare, some days feel like you just have to get through them, which can be a success in itself! Allow each day to be a reset for certain things. Some challenges will still be waiting for you tomorrow, and if you caused strife yesterday, that will not just magically disappear overnight. There are times when I experience a particularly tough day, through no obvious consequence of my actions, or inaction. This usually happens when I just do not understand what is happening. In such situations (where possible), I have learned that by going to bed early, I just leave 'it' behind mentally and start the next day with a fresh perspective. Try it!

Zoom out

Step back and look at the bigger picture. A day is a unit of time you can use and invest in to develop, grow, build something for yourself, and support others' dreams to be realised. When scrutinising a single day in isolation, it may seem unfruitful. However, when you connect it to a collection of days, you can compare it to solving a puzzle. Piece by piece, a larger picture begins to emerge. If we just look at one puzzle piece on its own, it rarely makes sense. We are unlikely to recognise the full image it contributes to. Every day can be another step towards a new beginning or future.

So, although you may not accomplish everything you want to in one day, do something towards what you want to achieve. It may be having a conversation, reading a book, or completing an application, and gradually, with consistency, a bigger 'something' will start to take shape and be revealed.

Here today, gone tomorrow!

The value of time was reinforced to me through my dad's sudden death. One day, he was around, and the next, he was gone. The plans and activities he still wanted to do are no longer possible for him (not that he is bothered about that now). He is loved very much, and although there was no time for final words, my last interaction with him was enjoyable. His life on earth stopped, but his influence lives on here through the legacy of great memories, values, and the good examples he invested in our family because he spent time developing his character and giving to others.

If quality time with family or friends is a value you have identified as important to you, great self-leadership will ensure you regularly spend time with those near you in meaningful ways. Good memories and experiences are the most valuable commodities we can leave behind when we pass on.

>>Think about it for a moment:

Can you identify one way to make more of the time you have?

What could be the next meaningful moment you create for someone?

How quickly do you recognise whether you are in a 'force' or 'flow' stance for the day?

Inputs & influencers

Are you managing your inputs and those to whom you give your attention? The sources of information you allow into your world influence your thinking, emotions, and decisions. Do you simply turn on the TV, radio, or browse social media, watching and listening to whatever image, conversation, opinion, or song is broadcast? Do you lack discernment as to whether this will boost your mood and guide your thoughts to something productive and useful towards where you are growing? You may not view it this way, but those you 'follow' on social media are 'leading' you somewhere. As you consume what they are posting, you allow them to lead your visual stimuli, influence your thinking, and shape your attitude, perspectives, etc. This is another crucial area where we can be intentional to maximise our time and focus.

Examine what channels of information are communicating with you, who you give time to, and their message. Check if these are from reliable sources that provide information, moving you closer to where you want to go and the person you want to become. Is there a mix of channels and voices with conflicting values? Are the good inputs being diluted by those of lesser value?

> Those you 'follow' on social media are 'leading' you somewhere.

A good habit to develop is to periodically review your inputs. Over time, as we grow and develop, our focus can change; therefore, the inputs that once served us well may no longer be appropriate. Do you follow too many people out of fear of missing out? Is their message still relevant to you?

The family members and friends closest to us influence us greatly. A huge benefit to me has been growing up in a family that demonstrates and pursues living selflessly. My parents and some other family members adopted this perspective and lifestyle when I was very young. Now, that does not mean that I (or they) automatically get it right all the time. However, this influence, which is still prevalent today, has helped to shape my perspective, given me tangible examples of acts of selflessness, and served to 'pull me up' when I have dropped my level of thinking to just myself. This has also influenced the friends I have built into my world and the type of friend I am to them. Are your friendships based solely on what you receive from them regarding support, encouragement, etc.?

'Walk with the wise and become wise; associate with fools and get in trouble.' [34]

Do you have family members or friends who demonstrate great self-leadership from a selfless perspective? If not, start intentionally reaching out to and connecting with those you see leading themselves well, where selfless acts are evident. Do your role models share similar values to yours? If not, I would suggest finding those that do. Perhaps you are in a work or family environment that mostly does not provide positive input (whether to the point of selflessness or just good self-leadership). In this case, be proactive and change or influence what you can. In addition, ensure that you find enough positive input elsewhere and that the level of this exceeds the amount of negative input the uncontrollable factors provide.

>>Think about it for a moment:

What are you allowing to influence you currently - positively and negatively?

What input(s) are you going to stop?

What input(s) will you increase and give more time to?

What input(s) are you going to add?

Consistency

Consistency is already evident in aspects of your life, but are you consistently doing good or bad things? Successful self-leaders leverage the power of consistency because they realise that consistency compounds. They make the day-to-day work for them. Consistency, when used well, can avoid the feeling of being overwhelmed and enable the production of certain outcomes that would be impossible in the short term. Imagine you wake up tomorrow morning with a burning desire to get six-pack abs. Unless you are already pretty toned, it will take time to develop them by exercising your abdominal muscles and possibly making some dietary changes. It would be unrealistic to achieve them in one day, regardless of how many crunches or other exercises you did. However, if you plan out a focused exercise schedule and ensure you eat the right amount of the right foods, your six-pack will become evident over time if you are consistent on both fronts. You will then need to stay consistent with an exercise or nutritional routine that will support you in maintaining these. That is how you can get consistency working for you.

Similarly, if you wanted to build a brick wall and were skilled in this area, you could complete it in a day, depending on the size. But if you only had limited time per day to devote to this and only added one new brick every day, eventually, if you stayed consistent, you would still complete the wall. Whatever the endeavour, you will see progress, provided your consistency level exceeds the rate of resistance against you. A year or five years from now, looking back, what would you wish you had been more consistent with?

Repetition and routine

These are close partners with consistency and habits. As consistency compounds, repetition reinforces. To expand our potential, we must value, implement, and utilise repetitive elements in life, which is easier once we realise their true worth. Think about a nutritional parallel as an example. While we have access to a wide variety of foods to consume, we regularly need to eat the same type of foods to continue to replenish the nutrients that build health and physical resilience in our bodies. How often do you eat the same type of food? Why? Because you have either developed an appetite for these or realise they are healthy and will contribute to your well-being.

> Consistency compounds; repetition reinforces.

Variety can invigorate and spice up our routines, so get creative to avoid things feeling 'stale'.

After repeatedly doing something, if the activity no longer stimulates or challenges us, we lose the enjoyment and plateau because we have raised our level of thinking, exertion, and experience to maintain that routine. In short, our interest plummets. We become demotivated, and continuing it in the same way becomes boring. At this point, we are likely to stop the activity unless we reinvigorate it with a change requiring a new kind or level of effort. Do your routines regularly require you to stretch yourself and experience something new? If not, make some changes to leverage the full benefit they can bring. Some routines can benefit initially, but if not reviewed, they may lead to stagnation, stifling creativity and spontaneity. Is there a routine you currently have that has become stale and needs reviving (because it could still be beneficial)? What will you do to add variety or freshen it up?

The power of repetition has potential in different areas of personal growth and leadership. We regularly need to be challenged with new things, new ways of behaving, and new ways of thinking to stay flexible and adapt when required. We also need to realise and embrace the importance of regularly revisiting elements we have heard, learnt, and studied previously. It is necessary to consume them afresh, never navigating away from the basics but building on them.

Have you ever read the same book more than once? If not, it is likely because you mentally ticked that off as 'completed' when you finished reading it. Wisdom has many levels of understanding. But when we allow thoughts like, *'I've heard this already…I know this'*, to stop us from listening to something we need to hear again, things that would sharpen our awareness or revive the practice of it in our daily activities, we stunt the opportunity to grow. ' *'I know that'* thoughts usually rob us of learning and improving in the moment. Often, when we rehear or reread something, it builds on the foundation of understanding laid previously and brings a greater depth of awareness and insight, which can then be translated into better goals or behaviours (if we are open to it).

[See also More of less?]. Although sometimes we just need the proverbial slap in the face to wake us up to something we let slip!

The negative effects of routine can most poignantly be recognised in those struggling with addictions, where routine actions towards substances or certain activities have a compounding effect that is harmful, negative, or ultimately destructive. A less obvious example would be to routinely criticise a friend or spouse. Over time, this negativity erodes their confidence and undermines trust within the relationship. If left unaddressed, distance and possibly separation will be the result.

Routines can be a really powerful benefit if we intentionally develop and establish those that serve what we want to achieve because they can exploit the qualities of consistency and repetition. Developing certain routine activities to the point where they become habits will enable them to run on 'auto-pilot'. These are then the new default, 'normal' level we live in and build from. Just 'rinse and repeat'. *[See also Habits]*. But there is a difference between habits and routines. Not every routine will necessarily become a habit. Habits run from the subconscious, so they can become almost effortless, whereas routines usually require intentional effort.

A case in point

I wrote the majority of the first draft of this book by spending 30 minutes a day (Mon - Fri) consistently for a prolonged period. I purposely did not set a hard and fast deadline to complete the book. This was not procrastination. Despite having written multiple blogs and posts, as this is my first full publication, I wanted my writing to grow organically with a certain amount of self-imposed pressure and within useful but not rigid boundaries of time and effort. It was also during this period that I wrote the 'Self-Leadership' chapter in *8 Qualities for Great Leadership*,[35] the collaborative book project I participated in with several other leaders. Concurrent with these activities, I was also taking book writing courses. This daily time period of writing became manageable amongst the mix of other activities, both personal and professional. Another benefit was the daily dopamine hit from achieving 30 minutes of writing! There were some sessions where I wrote less, thought through ideas more, or did some research, but the specific block of time during that period consistently enabled my creativity and self-expression to breathe and build.

Not another meeting

Do you lead or participate in boring meetings that follow the same agenda with little to no creativity or variance? What if these became the highlight of your team's day? Where everyone looks forward to getting together. Being creative may not come as naturally to you as to others, but it does not take much to start and involving a colleague for support and input could help. While there will no doubt be regular areas to discuss, how the discussion happens or the format, order, and input for these can vary. If you really want to get the best from your team, keep it interesting, engaging, and stimulating so that they look forward to the meeting starting rather than ending! Then, the routine will continue to work for you.

Remember to stretch

One evidence of successful self-leadership is when we have stretched ourselves to do something uncomfortable and stayed consistent with it so that it becomes routine. Think of one activity that was once difficult or uncomfortable, which you have now developed into a routine. Celebrate that win!

Some routines only serve us for a season(s). Therefore, as part of your self-reflection time, it is valuable to periodically assess the appropriateness of your current routines. When we consistently continue a routine that no longer serves us, it works against us. It is easier and more comfortable (in some ways) to stay with the familiar routines because we feel in control. They are more predictable than starting something new, but we know that if we want change, we need to change.

Something different needs to happen for something different to happen

> \>\>Think about it for a moment:
>
> Pause and evaluate! Which are the most important routines you currently have?
>
> Can you identify one routine that is counterproductive and you need to change it?
>
> What steps could you take to leverage the power of consistency more to your advantage?

Habits

How many habits do you have? That is a rhetorical question, but if you tried to identify and list each one, how long would it take? We are amazingly designed to be able to 'program' our subconscious mind with learned behaviours so it can process or 'run' these unconsciously in the background. In contrast, our conscious mind, which has less working capacity, focuses on the task or situation at hand.

Have you ever started making coffee while conversing with a family member? When you are familiar with the process, you can fill the kettle, put the coffee in the cup, add milk, etc., all without losing the flow of the conversation. Why? Because your subconscious is running the 'make coffee' programme while your conscious mind is listening to and processing the words you are hearing and inspiring you with words to converse. However, if you had just purchased a coffee machine and never used it before, you would have to pause the conversation, learn how to operate it, where to place the pod, how to fill the water reservoir, etc., until you had done this often enough that it became 'second nature'. Your conscious mind would not be able to focus well on learning how to operate the coffee machine AND have an engaging conversation at the same time unless it was about how to use a coffee machine!

The danger arises when we allow unintentional bad thinking, a lack of self-control, repetition, or environmental influence to program habits that do not serve us. Once established, these learned behaviours will run until confronted and addressed, then replaced by the intentional habits we want operating in our lives. Now, that may all sound complex; in some ways, it is, but it is all within our capability to control. That is why I am an advocate of coaching because this is an avenue where we get empowered to think about, explore, reveal, identify, and change the habits we no longer want to operate in. Coaching raises our level of conscious self-awareness *[see also Why Coaching is Transformative]*. I once had a client struggling with staying focused on her training preparation for a series of workshops because she had allowed the habit of looking at her phone whenever it buzzed with a notification. These frequent interruptions kept her from operating in flow, and therefore, the activity felt fragmented and laborious (even though she loved the content she was preparing!). Can you relate to a similar experience?

> We are amazingly designed to be able to 'program' our subconscious mind with learned behaviours.

Incorporating mindfulness techniques can also 'centre' us in the present to see things as they really are 'now' and recognise the current 'autopilot' activities to identify areas for change. But by definition, we cannot develop mindfulness activities on autopilot, as that defeats their purpose!

When you are developing new habits, give yourself some time to get them to the 'autopilot' stage. The first time we try, most new things will be less than perfect. Give yourself the space to learn, grow, and adapt. It is better to replace current habits with new ones of higher value rather than just trying to stop your current habits. The old ones will fade as new ones supersede them, and automaticity is established.

Stack a few

Linking or 'stacking' a few habits together can compound the benefits and return on our initial efforts to establish them, with exponential benefits realised from our consistency in keeping them. A simple example I use regularly, which stacks several habits, is when:

1. I utilise the Pomodoro technique and set a timer for 30 minutes, which I spend on focused activity, i.e., writing this book.

2. At the end of the 30 minutes, I go for a short walk (to give myself a break from looking at the screen and to give my body more movement and exercise).

3. When I walk, I use the affirmation, '*every time I walk, I get inspired*'. Most times, when I am walking, I get an idea or a way to develop something further that I have started. I will capture it using an app on my phone or as soon as I return to focused activity. The sooner I capture it, the better. This is because I have discovered that when I repeat an idea to myself to remember to write it down, I feel like I have 'clogged' the flow of inspiration and am hindering more ideas from surfacing.

4. While walking, I can also incorporate the 'boxed breathing' technique to regulate my physiology and lower any level of stress I may be experiencing.

There are a multitude of ways and variations that you can link habits together. First, identify new habits you want to establish, and then see how to link a few together. I have found calendar reminders to be a helpful trigger when forming a new habit. Whatever triggers or cues you decide to use, realise that these will need refreshing regularly as the familiar becomes hidden in plain sight. Once we get used to seeing the trigger but have not yet established the desired behaviour related to the trigger as a habit engrained in our subconsciousness, the effectiveness of the visual stimuli deteriorates. Eventually, it becomes ineffective in prompting our awareness to take the associated action. Depending on the intensity of the tasks or actions, you may find that linking 2-3 habits is sufficient at any given time. The key is not to link too many and feel overwhelmed. Find out what your tolerance is and work accordingly.

>>Think about it for a moment:

Identify one key habit working for you towards what you want to achieve.

Identify one new habit that you would like to implement. How could this be linked to the habit identified above?

Are there any habits that are no longer working for you?

Work/Activity

What are you doing? Are you doing these activities because nothing else is happening, or are you being specific and clear about how you want to spend your time and taking corresponding actions?

Are you leveraging the principle of causality (the relationship between cause and effect)?

How could 'now' be better?

Life is not just about doing 'stuff' and staying occupied, but doing the right stuff! Making work and activity your ally stems from discerning between what you 'could' do and what you 'should' do. Is there a good exchange between your time and energy and what you are experiencing and achieving? Do you feel stuck in a job or role that is restricting?

The Law of Priorities in *The 21 Irrefutable Laws of Leadership* states: *'...activity is not necessarily accomplishment'*.[36] This really made an impression on me when I read it because I know I enjoy *doing* things. Getting 'hands-on' and involved in tasks comes naturally to me, so I must regularly stay intentional about prioritising what I do, being clear that the outcome of any activity justifies my time. Are the activities you currently engage in (within and outside of 'work') attracting or producing your desired outcome? If you do not like or want the effects of your endeavours, adjust what is causing them!

Whether you own a business or are an employee, have you calculated your approximate hourly rate based on your working hours to salary/income ratio? You could use this to evaluate if the exchange of your time is worth the amount received. The worth of an activity can be measured in other ways than just finance. This is just an example to get you thinking. What value does this give your time? Is that acceptable? Is this value reflected in how you spend your time elsewhere?

Work smarter, not harder

> How could 'now' be better?

Are you making your time count when it comes to working as efficiently as possible? While analysing every move we make can become paralysing and, therefore, counterproductive, I believe regularly checking what and how we are doing something keeps us open to change. I remember hearing Bob Proctor state that the best way to do anything has not been invented yet. That got my attention!

Here are a few things to consider:

- Can you improve your state (mood, posture, etc.) before you start the task?
- Can you utilise technology and automation more?
- Are your activity areas free from distractions and hindrances?
- Do you capture ideas even when they surface at the most 'inconvenient' times?
- Are you ignoring rest breaks?
- Is a specific task taking longer than it needs to?

- Are there tasks you can outsource or actually stop doing?

Having a strong work ethic balanced between getting involved when you should and delegating tasks to others where appropriate is essential to accomplishing your goals well and effectively leading others.

To a large extent, life is what we make it. In my experience, opportunities rarely appear out of nowhere, unlinked to actions or connections I have been involved with. There is *something* related to them.

You can reach heights others will fail to attain if you put in the work that others will not

However, taking work to an extreme will result in burnout, which is really energetic or mental bankruptcy. Getting to this point renders you ineffective until recovery has taken place.

>>Think about it for a moment:

How balanced would you rate your current level of activity to be with regards to:

i) intentional focus on elements that will bring desired accomplishments?

ii) a healthy level of effort or time invested?

iii) doing what you 'should' rather than what you 'could' do?

What measures or indicators do you have in place that will provide useful warnings to prevent burnout?

"Evaluate your self-leadership,
not by the amount of wealth you amass,
but by the treasure you place in others' lives"

CHAPTER EIGHT

A moment to pause...

How are you doing? Remember the definition of self-leadership mentioned earlier:

'Doing what is most beneficial when you need to do it and choosing to be happy about it!'

Let us break this down a bit more now that we are this far into the book.

'Doing what is most beneficial...

- What do you need to do?
- What do you want to do?
- What do you need to find out?
- What could you implement or change?
- Who do you need to involve or approach?
- What resource do you need to provide or utilise?
- Where do you need to grow?
- What do you need to communicate?
- What is the best form for this communication?

...when you need to do it,

- What is the optimal time to do the aspects identified above?
- What activities have a critical deadline to be started or achieved? *[because of the knock-on effects if these do not happen].*
- What obstacles could delay these?

...and choosing to be happy about it!'

- Where could you be more emotionally intelligent regarding these?
- What would improve your feelings?
- What other areas would benefit as a by-product of you deciding to be positive or happy about these things?
- Who else would benefit?

CHAPTER NINE

Six Benefits of Self-Leadership

Are you a wise investor of your resources? The 'why' for good self-leading is driven by a desire to maximise our potential and live to our fullest state, knowing that others will also benefit the most when we do. Here are some of the benefits that motivate us to invest effort into developing healthy self-leadership. These are the by-products or rewards of aligning ourselves with the values and attitudes we want to express and then keeping ourselves living and leading in this arena.

1. Controlling what you can

Realising that we are not always able to do what we want comes with maturity, but the trade-off for this is easier when we realise that there are certain things we can control. However, are we ever really that in control? The answer is paradoxical, both 'yes' and 'no'. We all experience times of feeling powerless, 'out of our depth', where we encounter an area in which we lack knowledge and experience. These times test our character and can build resilience when we view them correctly. These are opportunities to rise above and overcome. The alternative is to avoid them, shrink back, and give our power to another person or circumstance. These scenarios can be different from periods of stretching where we are intentionally out of our comfort zone to grow and develop in an area. When we feel powerless, frustration and hopelessness start to grow. But in reality, we are not powerless!

When we self-lead well, we are less passive, more decisive, and can take more control. We benefit more when we put ourselves in a better state, thereby enhancing our perspective and flexibility. This allows us to draw upon our internal resources to adapt and learn while also being open to utilising assistance from others. It will also help us to maximise the resources available to us.

We experience the feeling of powerlessness less often because we can control our responses based on healthy EQ and thinking, which are aligned with our foundational values. This allows us to make the best of any situation and take control, further building confidence. It will not guarantee that we avoid all challenges and uncomfortable scenarios. However, we will be able to lead and live through them in a better state, producing better results. This is in contrast to *'taking life as it comes'* or just *'letting life happen'*, because both of these approaches place us in a reactive stance, preventing us from purposefully releasing our potential. Instead, we should initiate, act, direct, guide, adapt, and achieve.

> You can lead yourself well in all major areas.

Taking the lead in what you can control enables your life to be filled with the things you want to do and experience because you make them happen. The more intentional we are in our growth and leadership, the more we accelerate our effectiveness, which automatically leads to higher levels of satisfaction.

You *can* lead yourself well in all major areas, and when you find a place where you lack a skill, you can choose to develop it using your self-control and discipline. You can also motivate yourself to establish habits that will enable consistency to produce the desired outcome.

Environment

Environments can constantly change, sometimes drastically but usually subtly, over a period of time. Hence, regular review is beneficial. I believe we are created to control our environment(s), locally or beyond. Environment has a really big influence on our well-being and how well we grow, think, and feel. To a large extent, we can control our environment. Do not let the aspects you cannot change prevent you from changing what you can. Think about how much we can create, build, and change an environment so that it is conducive to our growth where we study, socialise, work, etc. Is your current environment contributing to your well-being and growth? If not, what can you do differently? If it is, how could you enhance this further?

Some examples:

- If you enjoy sitting in the garden to reflect or study but have since moved to an apartment, could you visit a local park or just add some plants to your apartment?
- If you wanted to learn how to speak French, you would pick up the language quicker by living in a French-speaking country or community. This immersive environment would produce better results than if you were living in a German-speaking country or community.
- If you enjoy listening to music, adding this to a mundane or unpleasant task changes your environment and can lift your mood, making the task less onerous.
- Is there a particular scent or aroma you find relaxing or energising?

What would your ideal environment be? Lots of space with books, gadgets, or something more minimalistic? Is it filled with the ambience of a city and the hustle and bustle of people, or somewhere more remote, serene, and quiet? It could be that dwelling in a mix of these sometimes brings more balance. Once you have identified the environmental characteristics you prefer, consider what aspects you can control, incorporate, or change. If you would rate your current environment as a '6' (on a scale of 1-10), how could you enhance it to '8' or even '10'? The more our environment reflects healthy self-expression without encroaching on the freedoms of others, the more conducive it is to our productivity.

Then, consider the environment you have and are creating for those you lead. Some cultural aspects are covered in the '*Healthy teams*' section below. What resources, equipment, processes, etc., could be used to utilise more and improve the environment your team operates in? Ask for their ideas and find out each member's ideal environment. This can promote effective learning and be a potent team-building exercise.

>>Think about it for a moment:

How much control do you have over your life right now?

Identify one area initially where you can begin to take more control. What is the first step to take?

What within your environment could you consciously improve?

- In your immediate environment? *[where you dwell/operate in/from]*

- In your local environment? *[in your community]*

- In your wider environment? *[in your locality, region, or further afield]*

---

2. Attract high-calibre people

A crucial factor that determines the level of success you achieve is the quality or calibre of people you spend time with, both socially and professionally (associates, partners, team members). 'Iron sharpens iron, so one man sharpens another.'[37] We naturally gravitate towards those similar to ourselves in behaviours, passions, interests, outlook, values, etc., and it is easier to build a healthy connection with those who share common ground. But we also need individuals in our lives who are different in ways that will stretch us to grow positively.

As you continue to lead yourself better, you will attract people of higher calibre, those who are also investing in their own development with aligned values and pursuing a cause greater than themselves, because *you* have transitioned to a higher-calibre person. By default, you also naturally distance yourself from lower-calibre people. Lower-calibre people do not have lesser value as individuals but have less value to contribute to who you are becoming or what you are looking to achieve. That is not to say we should not help or spend time with those who are different from us. However, we will thrive more and maximise our potential the more we surround ourselves with people who are intentionally raising their leadership and growing personally.

Note: There needs to be balance, e.g., our team members may not all be at the same level of experience or pace of growth as ourselves. Team diversity is a vital ingredient to success, and good self-leaders are intentional about balancing the depth and breadth of experience and perspectives within their teams. Thus, a 'high-calibre' person may not necessarily be more advanced in their leadership journey than you. They may be an excellent team member who is willing to take responsibility and support what you are doing. Similarly, a high-calibre person may not be extremely wealthy, as quality or success is not always measured or defined this way. It could be that they have an excellent understanding of a certain area or have developed a high level of proficiency or insight regarding something valuable to you.

Leading and following

> We intuitively know when to 'step up' and take the lead, and when to 'sit down' and listen.

We are all searching for great leaders to follow in certain areas who will empower us to progress in life. And we are also looking for great followers—those with aligned values and an attitude to serve the vision or purpose we are pursuing. People will want to be around you more when you lead well and value others.

Another paradox that works in our favour is that when you become a better leader, you become a better follower. Also, when you become a better follower, you become a better leader.

When I look at the leaders in my life, they are also good followers. They are serving someone on a 'higher level'. By that, I mean they serve someone with more influence or a bigger purpose who has a bigger vision and is more experienced or competent. It means someone further along the leadership journey than themselves.

We all need to lead, and we all need to follow. There are some things that we should not lead on but follow the direction of others because they are better equipped or positioned to do so. Healthy self-leadership means we intuitively know when to 'step up' and take the lead and when to 'sit down' and listen so that we can follow well.

>>Think about it for a moment:

Who have you currently drawn towards your sphere of influence and what you are pursuing?

How could you be more intentional about attracting people of higher calibre?

Who are you intentionally following?

How could you follow more effectively?

Can you identify an area where you must 'step up' or 'sit down'?

---

3. Healthy teams

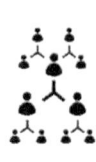

You can maximise productivity and effectiveness because healthy teams leverage the exponential potential and ability of the skills and talents of many. High-performing teams are greater than the sum of their parts.

Self-leadership is a valuable asset and positions you well in teams because it makes you a better team player and leader. You are not pursuing your own agenda, which squashes others to make you look good or serves your needs and detracts from others. Likewise, you will avoid 'hanging another team member out to dry' to deflect from accepting personal responsibility for your actions and to put the blame on someone else.

As a team member, you contribute to influencing the atmosphere in a healthy way because your focus is on giving and fortifying the well-being of the team as a whole. You take personal responsibility not just for your actions but to ensure others are equipped and supported to contribute well to achieve goals (whether in a self-managed team or not). Your self-leadership level will also support the leader's vision. You become a more valuable asset to them because you focus on the bigger picture and can identify issues and offer solutions to make necessary adjustments. If we apply the Pareto principle here as a guide, where 80% of a team's results come from the top 20% of producers, developing quality self-leadership increases our ability to be in the top 20%.

As a team leader, you are the 'thermostat' determining the overall atmosphere that the team operates in. Although everyone plays a part, you are the biggest contributor to the team culture. When you lead yourself well, you will lead others positively and consistently because you stay focused and consciously keep the vision in view. Your communication will align with the vision, and everyone will feel united, knowing their purpose, where they are going, and how their skills or efforts contribute to the cause. Your behaviour will not be unpredictable, bringing assurance, security, and building trust. Operating at a high level of EQ means you will not pass your stress and frustrations on to others.

> High-performing teams are greater than the sum of their parts.

Be authentic

People want to follow others who have great values and behave well. That does not mean you cannot show emotion or must be perfect, but the better we lead ourselves, the more naturally we demonstrate the right behaviours and responses. Do not be afraid to be honest about mistakes or to show the appropriate level of vulnerability. Your team must know you are real, authentic, and much like them! (Honesty does not mean full disclosure about everything. It needs to be mixed with discretion). Vulnerability and openness build a higher level of trust. Leaders can make the mistake of thinking that admitting mistakes or being vulnerable equates to weakness, which will undermine a team's security. This is not the case; incompetence does this! Leaders lead, so if you want to nurture a healthy environment of trust and openness, you must be vulnerable first.

By continuing your own growth, you will be more open to developing other team members and building a conducive environment to expand their abilities and experience. **Note**: When the team is functioning well, it is tempting to keep things as they are, but at some point, you need to release your best people and let them move on. Do not put a lid on their growth and potential. If you hold on to them for too long, you will lose them anyway, or they will regress and perform below their potential.

>>Think about it for a moment:

[As a team leader] If the health of your team was audited on a scale of 1-10 (with 10 being optimal health), how well do you think it would rate?

What could you do to increase this rating, whatever the current score is?

Are you ensuring there is the appropriate level of fun within activities, meetings, etc.?

> [As a team member] Where could you 'step up' and improve your communication, approach, and perspective towards the team's vision?
>
> How could you support the team leader and individual members more?

4. Maximising opportunities

There are a plethora of opportunities available to us at any given time if we are aware enough to see them. We cannot necessarily engage with all of them, but are we choosing the right ones to invest our time, focus, and energy into?

One of the benefits of being clear and focused about where you want to go and setting goals that align with this is that these goals help filter out opportunities that may actually be 'good' but not 'great' for where you are or the destination you are working towards.

Opportunities are there to be utilised. Some are time-bound, and if we try to save them for later (or when we feel more ready), they may have passed or died. Leading ourselves well empowers us to respond more effectively in the moment, but when we are not in the right state, place, or level of conscious awareness, we can miss out. Have you ever felt the disappointment of seeing an opportunity, but for one reason or another, you did not take it, and then it passed, and the window closed? Missing opportunities may not necessarily be life or death, but they could cost us financially or in another area. Add to this the reality that opportunities are pregnant with potential, and some are buried within others; therefore, they only become available or evident once we have embraced the initial opportunity. This can mean that the actual cost of missing these is greater than it first seems.

The better we self-lead, the more empowered we are to create opportunities. I am convinced that if we do not step out and do certain things, they will just not happen. But new possibilities arise as we grow and continue to move beyond the familiar and comfortable. Is it that they have always been there waiting for us and that we have now positioned ourselves to embrace them?

Think about your relationships. How many people have you met through other people that you have met? What if you had not taken the opportunity to meet the first person? What is the likelihood that you would have then met the people that they later introduced you to? Maybe you would have, maybe not. If you take this to an extreme, you can become anxious about missed opportunities that have disappeared, and you cannot do anything about it. That is not a helpful approach to adopt. Instead, realise that by leading ourselves well, we are positioned to benefit from taking the right opportunities and maximising them.

> How many people have you met through other people that you have met?

Have you met…?

I had a great conversation with a podcast guest who, when we were chatting afterwards, mentioned that she wanted to write a book. I immediately remembered a conversation I had with a friend the same week who had mentioned meeting a book coach on a recent podcast. We were able to connect them, and I later discovered that they were working together to write her book! It was satisfying because it aligns with my goal of empowering others to be more successful, and it also illustrates the point about opportunities appearing through our connections with others.

We may cross paths with some people briefly and then continue on our journey in life. What effect are we having on these brief interactions? Are the majority positive, negative, or mediocre?

Creating opportunities for others

While leading a team of volunteers at a conference, I adopted the habit of intentionally looking for others on the team to whom I could give responsibilities. This has now been my default perspective for a long time: to enable individuals to develop their leadership skills by creating opportunities for them to 'step up'. This also relies on the decision on their part to utilise the moment. One lady, in particular, appeared somewhat surprised when I asked her to look after a certain task. However, she responded to my belief in her abilities and became deeply involved. Remarkably, she got into the flow of activity and ran some tasks with the team better than I had thought to do. So, the team was more efficient, and we all benefitted! We then had further conversations about her taking on more leadership elements. That is what it is all about!

>>Think about it for a moment:

Take a few moments to list four people who have significantly impacted your personal life, business, or leadership journey…

1.   2.   3.   4.

How many of these were introduced to you by someone you met outside your normal sphere of influence?

What opportunities are you currently creating that are contributing to developing others?

---

5. Making a positive difference

Leading ourselves well primarily contributes positively to our well-being in how we think, behave, view others or circumstances, and make life better!

We cannot experience true fulfilment in the absence of self-leadership. We are the first to benefit from aligning ourselves well with our values and controlling what we can. It brings ease, balance, and peace. Although it does not correct everything misaligned all at once and may not solve every problem we experience, it places us in an optimum state to lead from. The better we feel, the more we smile and naturally infuse our environments with positivity. The more we adopt the right attitude of living beyond ourselves and doing good, the more we train our brains and shape our perspective to attract and see more opportunities to be a positive influence.

Early on in my leadership journey, I realised that leadership is a lot about taking initiative and making something happen. You will see things that others do not see. It is very satisfying and motivating when you realise that if you had not acted on something you saw, it may well have been left undone. But because you acted, things improved. Leaders set the pace and tone within teams and will naturally initiate directly or by collaborating with others. You *can* make a positive difference and use your influence to benefit others and make the world a better place.

> We cannot experience true fulfilment in the absence of self-leadership.

Look around

Some people are making positive contributions to their world and communities, and you too can! I am certain there are issues or things (large or small) you encounter that bother you, where you want to see change or believe a different approach would be more beneficial.

- What do you see that is not being done but could be?
- Are you waiting for 'the government' to do something about it?
- Do you hear yourself say that 'they' (whoever they are) should not have let this happen or that it is their responsibility?

These can be signs of things you could take the lead on or get involved in to instigate change. There may be small things that would benefit from your input. It does not have to involve major change, although it might. You may hold the idea that unlocks a perceived impasse, starts a new initiative, or brings enhancement by releasing a new level of creativity or efficiency. The potential is huge!

What if we lived with the intention that wherever we go, things are better afterwards?

Can you see examples in others where better self-leadership would have contributed to better outcomes? Use your findings not to judge others but to learn and enquire within where or whether you have similar traits or are producing comparable results.

How can you make others successful, or even more so? Or is your passion less in supporting others to build a business or reach the wealth levels they desire and better expressed more compassionately in helping the homeless to get on the ladder of recovery from addiction, rejection, self-harm, etc.? There is definitely a place for all of us to get involved somehow in contributing to causes like this. If we were in their shoes, we would want someone to help us, right? For some, being 'hands-on' or helping financially could be the most effective way of getting involved.

>>Think about it for a moment:

What do you notice that others seem oblivious to or are indifferent towards?

What is it that bugs you and you want to change?

Is there space to do this without subverting someone else's authority?

---

6. Establishing a legacy

What will remain *after* you have breathed your last breath? What will you have passed on? Depending on which stage of your life you consider yourself to be at currently, it is likely to determine how much thought you have given to these questions up to this point. Is it something you will get to when you are older?

But do you really know how long you will live?

What are you intentionally choosing to leave as your legacy?

Legacy does not have to be a morbid subject. Think generationally. What can you start and pass on for others to continue afterwards? Life, as we know it, is short. Great self-leadership not only puts us in the driving seat of our lives and heading in the direction we want to travel but also keeps us thinking outwardly, on a larger scale, and releases higher levels of creativity. We can make more changes and instigate new initiatives than when we live with poor self-leadership. Start today to think and plan what you want to do now, which will continue when you leave it behind. As Paul Scanlon teaches, learn to '*live full but die empty*',[38] by investing yourself in others and passing on your wisdom, insights, and experiences. Those that follow should stand on our shoulders rather than start at the same level we did.

> We will all leave and pass on something.

Your legacy will be linked to your values. What would make your life count? If you value building large or multiple businesses for your children to inherit, this will determine how you will focus your time and energy. Some reading this may want to make a name for themselves and be remembered for their achievements by generations to come as the person who invented or discovered 'XYZ' or set a world record. Whether you desire to leave a grand legacy or something you consider more 'medium-sized', we will all leave and pass on something. To me, that energises me to continue to grow myself, build, support, and develop the lives of others. I want to make the most of my time here with my life, contributing to a higher purpose and the success and expansion of others, be it family, friends, clients, or people with whom I may only have a short interaction.

If these examples sound lofty to you, maybe you prefer to remain 'in the background' and are energised less by being known or building an empire but more by building a healthy home and raising your children with good values, who then pass these on to your grandchildren. This, to me, is commendable and just as important. This, then, is what you should focus on. I believe we decide the level of influence and legacy we leave based on our intentions and willingness to grow. When you look back on your life, how will you answer the question:

Was it a life well lived?

Heart tattoos and digital expressions

We will all leave memories and experiences in the hearts and minds of those close to us and often to a wider circle. Great self-leadership ensures these are positive memories. These memories are sometimes those of when we loved and believed the best in others, when we succeeded or gave a hand, when we failed and got back up, and on occasions when we hurt people, apologised, and sought reconciliation. Every interaction with someone has the potential to really make an impression on them, to indelibly tattoo their heart, but will this be a good internal image that remains with them?

Does anything captured digitally really disappear? Is your self-expression on social media contributing to building a positive legacy? Often, posts and content are still visible after someone dies and can be a lasting memory or snapshot of how you lived and expressed your uniqueness. This increases when you appear on others' channels, too. Pause for a moment and scroll back over your recent content:

- If these became your last words, are they communicating what you want to pass on?
- Is this how you want to be remembered?
- Could this avenue be used more intentionally to effectively empower others, continue your purpose, and further your message beyond your years here, amongst the fun of enjoying and expressing moments?

Legacy does not have to be serious but genuine and authentic. Intentional communication and actions can contribute more to a well-lived life. As innovative technology continues to evolve, with an increasing capacity to leverage new possibilities, how can you use the current and future communication channels better?

What will you be remembered for?

For me, as well as the positive internal and external changes I assist in facilitating through coaching and training, this book is another expression of what I am intentionally leaving behind for others. Decide what you want to leave and then allow that to motivate you and give you a 'second wind' to persevere through the tough times. Leverage the legacy benefits of developing and operating in high-quality self-leadership that expands the influence of your life to positively affect others. This can be an inspiration for them to do the same.

>>Think about it for a moment:

On a scale of 1-10 (10 = extremely intentional, 1 = not thought about it), how intentional have you been so far in thinking about what legacy you want to leave?

Based on your highest core values, what does your ideal legacy look like?

What next step can you take to establish the legacy you want to leave?

What do you need to devise and implement a strategic plan to realise this?

"Selfless self-leadership is the highest form of leadership"

CHAPTER TEN

Why Coaching is Transformative

Misunderstanding authentic coaching and the power of a strategic partnership will steal MASSIVE growth from you. Do you really want to miss out?

"Fantastic, I've come alive and have more energy than when I started the session."

"I feel so much more positive and energised. I am clearer about getting rid of the obstacles [fear, etc]. Thank you for a superb session."

Having referred to coaching experiences and benefits in earlier chapters, I wanted to elaborate and explain them in more detail. Incorrect preconceived ideas or a misconception of the purpose and mechanics of the coaching process blind us to the innate wealth of resources available to us from our subconscious mind and our ability to utilise them more. BUT I also want you to know that working with a coach is not essential to developing your self-leadership skills to some degree. However, it will enhance and expedite growth and can determine the extent of your progress in areas where you want to thrive. It can take you further than if you choose to pursue self-leadership alone. Coaching is a powerful catalyst for releasing potential. 'Potential', by its very definition, does not mean inevitable!

Hiring a coach is not about getting hyped up or being artificially inspired by someone else. Inspiration and excitement are a few of the by-products of the coaching process, but the reason coaching is so transformative and a great return on investment is much deeper than that.

> 'Potential', by its very definition, does not mean inevitable!

Coaching covers ALL aspects of life because, even though we may think we can separate and compartmentalise different responsibilities and activities, they are all tied to one common thread: OURSELVES.

As the proverb states:

> *'Counsel in the heart of someone is like deep water, but a person of understanding will draw it out.'* [39]

I believe the 'person of understanding' refers to both the coach and coachee. We all possess the answers we need, but these are often buried under distractions and choked by disbelief or past failures. As the coachee, we can discover these hidden answers the more we seek them and are honest and open with our feelings and fears. And the coach works with us to facilitate and nurture this process of exploration and discussion.

As a coach, I empower individuals and groups to discover their own answers from within themselves. I am responsible for creating, facilitating, and collaborating with them in the discovery process. However, THEY are responsible for the level of honesty they reach and the actions they identify and commit to in order to benefit their lives and accelerate them towards their goals and dreams. It is an equal alliance between the individual(s) and the coach. The coach is not acting as a guru or instructor, so is therefore not limited to assisting only within their realm of experience. The coach and client work together on the <u>fundamental understanding</u>

that the client is the expert in their life, not the coach. THEY are keenly aware, more than anyone else, of what motivates them to take action, what thrills and delights them, and ultimately what they will take responsibility for.

Based on my experience, competence and passion, I operate predominantly as a leadership coach, empowering others to lead themselves well and lead others better, but coaching addresses the whole person. Therefore, even though my area of expertise is not health and fitness, or finance, these areas are not excluded, when appropriate, from how I assist clients to succeed because the principles are the same and areas are often interlinked. There may be value at times in seeking out coaches with specific expertise, although this is vital only when looking for a mentor.

"…tremendous. I've gained clarity in a lot of areas."

"I wouldn't really be pushing myself and stepping up if we didn't have these conversations."

If you could, you would, wouldn't you?

Leveraging the power of coaching not only accelerates your progress and success in the areas you know you want to develop but also provides an exploratory and discovery element that brings a new level of clarity, enabling you to set a laser focus on specific options identified that you want to progress. This gives you the edge—an advantage over others in your field who do not utilise and benefit from the transformation this external collaboration provides. I believe the MAIN REASON why more people do not utilise and leverage the power of coaching (it was the reason why I did not for many years) is ignorance of the power it brings.

A coaching session is so much more than a conversation. Talking through areas, ideas, dreams, obstacles, behaviours, outcomes, etc., is definitely part of the process. It is also about taking time and having the courage to really think, because having thoughts and intentional thinking are not the same. Thinking intentionally about reasons for behaviours and results, AND new options and approaches, bypasses our initial learned responses to 'the norm' that we usually allow to direct us. This is where we dig within ourselves to uncover the gold that, deep down, we hope or know is there but have been unwilling for one reason or another to mine for it.

Every time we invest in coaching, we work against our natural default inclination to stay comfortable and regress

Comfort is only beneficial for so long

"It was uncomfortable, but I'm glad we went there because that's how we grow."

"It's always helpful. It's not often I get to talk through some of this."

In safe hands

Having the freedom to explore, imagine, experiment, and think outside the box in a non-judgemental and confidential environment is a HUGE contributing factor to expanding our outlook. It sparks desires and inspiration that we subconsciously carry with us but which may never surface to our conscious level by themselves, or at least not frequently enough for us to pay attention to and respond to. Most of the time, sad to say, too many of the world's population underutilises the power of their imagination when it comes to really expanding perceived boundaries.

Are we living and thinking that our only options regarding a certain aspect are our first ideas or those listed on page 1 of a search result?

The coach collaborates to create a conducive environment that allows you to focus your time and attention on vital areas that the day-to-day routines and demands crowd out. Habits and limiting beliefs that have become so engrained within us that we just accept them as a 'part of who we are' can be exposed and addressed to move us into a more empowered and productive state. It is about giving ourselves time to be brutally honest with ourselves.

> When was the last time you had an honest conversation with yourself about where you are compared to where you want to be? Did you identify what was holding you back?

With raised self-awareness, we gain deeper insight, become sharper, and start to think differently, higher, and more creatively. This enables new ideas and actions to be embraced and planned. As with all areas of growth, there is a stretching involved where we move into new areas or intentionally prioritise things that we may not feel like doing over those we would rather do or naturally gravitate towards. That is why coaching works in partnership with self-leadership, because sometimes, we need encouragement and assistance to get out of our own way!

> *"This has given me more clarity and saved me some work."*
>
> *"Since our sessions together, I am a lot more intentional..."*
>
> *"...well pleased with the actions and the results of my commitments."*

Investing in ourselves to the point where we hold ourselves accountable to someone else sends a powerful internal signal to our self-belief. Also, it fortifies the desire to follow through with our intentions and the commitments we have made externally, to 'save face' and live with integrity. We can reinforce this by setting a specific time limit or 'do by' date, (which could coincide with your next coaching session, or at a time point of your choosing). The more we apply dates and times to when we will progress or complete actions, the more likely we are to prioritise them. These add clarity, provide impetus and an end point from which we can plan back from.

Coaching expedites growth

Looking to get the edge compared to others may not sound selfless, but as I said earlier, it is not about trying to be better than anyone else. It is about being better than I was yesterday—the best expression of ME possible at any moment. The better we develop ourselves, the better we can assist and empower others. The better we can empower others, the more value we add and the more satisfaction we experience (and so do they). For example, consider two business leaders. One intentionally develops their self-leadership to then empower others well, while the other does not. In this scenario, the individual pursuing growth and maximising opportunities for development for themselves and others will likely achieve a stronger level of success and productivity. There is something significant about involving others in our growth journey (provided they are the right people at the right time).

Coaching is NOT therapy

Coaching does not 'fix' individuals and is one aspect of many possible interventions we can embrace as we live, grow, and face life's challenges. Coaching focuses predominantly on your present and future aspects and aspirations, only visiting the past briefly to glean relevant information on an area of current or future focus. If you have problems with unresolved trauma from past events, the first step in moving forward from this may be to talk with a counsellor. But as that is not my field of expertise, please seek the appropriate professional(s) to direct you to the best approach. Coaching may then be the next beneficial step following that intervention.

"Really useful to get back on track after three weeks of chaos."

"I appreciate it. I don't talk about this stuff otherwise."

"Massively useful."

>>Think about it for a moment

How can you leverage the transformative power of coaching in your life to:

a. gain more clarity on who you want to become?

b. sharpen your focus on what you want to achieve and how to channel resources?

c. maximise your self-leadership and beyond?

"Gold is rarely found lying on the surface"

CHAPTER ELEVEN

Faith Does Not Mean Perfection

I hesitated to include this chapter, not because I am in any way ashamed of my faith or uncertain whether this viewpoint could help you. I believe it certainly can, but I have limited writing about this aspect because I know that some have different viewpoints. I do not want you to miss out on the valuable content of this book because of a difference in spiritual beliefs. I realise that some have 'leaked out' in previous chapters because it is part of who I am, and it is impossible to separate this from my leadership experiences and understanding. Therefore, I have written this chapter to explain a little about my perspective for those interested. To be like Christ demands the highest level of self-leadership, accompanied by grace and acceptance when we miss the mark.

Faith in Jesus Christ as Saviour and Lord has been fundamental to my life since childhood. It is about growing in a personal relationship with the Creator of our being, the universe, and everything in it. But my intention in including this is not to push my beliefs on you. These leadership principles and the benefits of selfless self-leadership are universal and influence many spiritual ideologies. They will work anywhere if applied with the correct motive, with anyone, regardless of culture or faith.

At times, as the Church is entrusted to communicate God's love to humanity, we fall short. Church leaders make mistakes, scandals are reported, abuse becomes evident, and people get hurt. Does that mean they are bad leaders? I think one of the wisest statements that brings the right perspective to me for this is, '*Let him who is without sin among you be the first to throw a stone...*'[40] Now, leaders set the standard of behaviour and have a higher expectation placed on them (and rightly so). There is a place where trust has been broken for leaders to step down or be removed from certain responsibilities for a season, maybe indefinitely, with criminal convictions to be applied if appropriate. Each case should be considered independently, wisely thought through, and prayed about to get God's direction on how to proceed. But think about it: are we really expecting leaders to be perfect? Where there is repentance, we can all experience God's grace to forgive our mistakes and bring restitution. There is always hope, regardless of the circumstances! (But the flip side is that it is not an excuse to be lazy, live selfishly, without discipline, or continue in sin).

> To be like Christ demands the highest level of self-leadership, accompanied by grace and acceptance when we miss the mark.

God is the Ultimate Leader, and as His ambassadors on the planet, we, the Church, are responsible for demonstrating and modelling great leadership from a place of selfless self-leadership. We do not always reflect and communicate God's unconditional love that we have experienced or show the true depth of forgiveness. This has regrettably caused hurt and true cries of "hypocrisy" inside and outside the Church.

I would encourage you not to judge God's love or desire to know YOU by the mistakes of His people

When we invite Jesus Christ into our hearts, we become Christians (people growing to become more like Christ). The transformative new life is then instantaneously birthed within us. We literally become 'new creations', new versions of ourselves, BUT this is the start of our journey to becoming more like Christ. We are forgiven, and God begins to work in us, by His Holy Spirit, to enable us to move on from our past mistakes, weaknesses, hang-ups, and baggage. We are able to forgive and overcome our insecurities and feelings of low self-esteem, fear etc. We are empowered to embrace and work through failures, trauma, abuse, etc., and serve Him and others by discovering, developing, and expressing the gifts He has placed within us.

The Christian walk, like selfless self-leadership, depends on our willingness to grow and cooperate with what we learn. At times, we can focus less on developing this, much to the detriment of our own happiness, and miss opportunities to benefit others. But we can resume developing our self-leadership at any point, from wherever we find ourselves.

Closing thoughts

The choice is yours

Successful self-leadership is voluntary; no one can force you to lead yourself optimally. It is about taking personal responsibility for every area of your life. You have the freedom to embrace it and live in the fullness it brings, with the option of enhancing this to selfless self-leadership—connected to and serving a purpose bigger than yourself. On the other hand, you can ignore everything in this book and just live and behave depending on how you feel at any given moment.

Should you be considering the latter, I would encourage you first to really think about and imagine how the rest of your life will likely turn out by default if you do, in all areas, including relationships, satisfaction, health, finance, etc.

With what I know, living from that perspective would be scary for me. How many individuals who have built something significant (rather than simply inherited wealth) did it by consistently serving themselves and living undisciplined, reacting to how they felt at any given moment? Remember:

We pass through this life only once...

What about now?

At any given moment, you need to decide how much effort you will invest in growing yourself and developing others. Up to this point in time, if you have not invested as much as you have wanted to, the best time to start to change that is now. Let the past serve as a teacher, not a jailer. Identify why this is so (and the beliefs behind it) and take an immediate, small step to start momentum in the desired direction and areas. Then, keep moving forward. Be intentional about planning to change this, and ensure you connect with others who will support and encourage you on your new path.

While reading this book, did you pause and think through the questions in the '>>Think about it for a moment' sections? If not, what was the reason? Were you too busy, or did you postpone doing this for another time? Remember, the level of focused time and effort we put into something directly affects the level of benefit and understanding we receive from it.

Maximise more

If you are already a high achiever and have experienced some level of success, how can you raise your game, shift gears, and take your awareness, skills, and influence to the next level? (Because there is always room for more). What can you scale?

Regardless of the measure we have of the elements mentioned in this book working in and through our lives, these, too, are largely unlimited. So, where can you expand, sharpen your focus more, and increase efficiencies?

In summary, great self-leadership:

- Confronts and tackles the hard stuff within us
- Gets comfortable with discomfort – regularly looking to stretch ourselves in growth areas
- Is aware of our state at all times
- Makes adjustments, not excuses
- Is fundamentally motivated by empowering others the best that we can

- Realises the importance of regular self-care
- Positions ourselves in the most optimal environments as often as possible
- Is always looking to grow and learn
- Leverages allies and resists enemies
- Maximises opportunities
- Differentiates between 'could do' and 'should do'
- Balances well the 'big picture' perspective with the 'here and now'

When we fail to lead ourselves well, we are not in the best position mentally, emotionally, relationally, or geographically to optimise opportunities and our potential.

Remember:

You decide whether you are, or become a great leader

>>Think about it for a moment:

Now that you have reached the end of this book…

What is the one most important adjustment you are going to make?

What is the first step in making this adjustment happen?

What action then follows this?

Over to you…

*I BELIEVE IN YOU
AND
I BELIEVE IN YOUR
POTENTIAL...*

YOU Lead You!

References

1. Paraphrased from Cambridge & Dictionary.com definitions.

2. 'Prosocial Spending and Well-Being', Aknin, L.B. and Hanniball, K. https://www.oxfordbibliographies.com/view/document/obo-9780199828340/obo-9780199828340-0193.xml [accessed 01/03/2022]

3. 'Altruism, happiness, and health: it's good to be good' Stephen. G. Post *International Journal of Behavioural Medicine* 12, 66-77 (2005) https://link.springer.com/article/10.1207/s15327558ijbm1202_4 https://pubmed.ncbi.nlm.nih.gov/15901215/ [both accessed 8/2/2022].

4. Eva Ritvo M.D. 2014 https://www.psychologytoday.com/gb/blog/vitality/201404/the-neuroscience-giving [accessed 14/4/22].

5. Wood, A. M., et al., Gratitude and well-being: A review and theoretical integration, *Clinical Psychology Review* (2010), doi: 10.1016/j.cpr.2010.03.005.

6. Simon Sinek, *The Infinite Game* (Penguin Random House LLC 2019), Ch 9

7. Thor's stepmother, ~90mins 40 secs into the movie, Avengers Endgame – Marvel Studios 2019.

8. Cited on the American Psychological Association website:

https://www.apa.org/news/press/releases/2012/08/lying-less [accessed 19/7/23].

9. '*Rest is Productive*', Max Frenzel May 27th 2020 https://betterhumans.pub/rest-is-productive-1348b2b7eeb0 [accessed 8/3/22].

10. Alex Soojung-Kim Pang, *Rest: Why You Get More Done When You Work Less,* cited by Emily Whitten: https://blog.trello.com/achieve-restorative-rest-productivity [accessed 8/3/22].

11. Ecclesiastes 12 v 12, *The Holy Bible*, New International Version, Biblica, Inc. Copyright ©1973, 1978, 1984, 2011.

12. David Walton, *A Practical Guide to Emotional Intelligence: Get Smart about Emotion* (Icon Books Ltd 2012) Pg 24, Kindle version.

13. Yeukai Business Show Podcast, https://pod.co/yeukai-business-show/episode-383-rebecca-schauer-how-to-break-free-from-cycles-of-over-stressing-and-stress-eating

14. Proverbs 16 v 32, *The Holy Bible,* Berean Study Bible, https://berean.bible/

15. John C. Maxwell, *Leadership Gold* (Thomas Nelson 2008), Ch. 17.

16. Cambridge Dictionary, https://dictionary.cambridge.org/dictionary/english/procrastination [accessed 4/3/22]

17. Risa Williams, *The Ultimate Time Management Toolkit: 25 Productivity Tools for Adults with ADHD and Chronically Busy People* (Jessica Kingsley Publishers 2022), Ch. 1, Pg 36.

REFERENCES

18. '*The Learning Stages*' were created by Noel Burch, co-author with Thomas Gordon of the Teacher Effectiveness Training book, 1974. https://www.gordontraining.com/leadership/four-stages-learning-theyre-circle-not-straight-line/ [accessed 3/8/23].

19. The '5 Whys' approach. Multiple online sources including, https://sixsigmastudyguide.com/5-whys/ [accessed 15/11/22].

20. Unconscious bias, further reading: https://www.imperial.ac.uk/equality/resources/unconscious-bias/ [accessed 1/11/2023].

21. DISC Behavioural Analysis - https://trevorstockwell.com/disc

22. American Psychological Association - https://www.apa.org/topics/research/multitasking [accessed 1/9/23].

23. Scripture taken from THE MESSAGE. NavPress Publishing Group. Copyright ©1993. 1994, 1995, 1996, 2000, 2001, 2002.

24. Dr. Caroline Leaf, *Cleaning Up Your Mental Mess* (Baker Books 2021), Ch. 9, Pg 194.

25. Napoleon Hill, *Think & Grow Rich* (Capstone Publishing Ltd 2009) Ch 11., Pg 286.

26. Sleep Foundation, https://www.sleepfoundation.org/physical-activity/athletic-performance-and-sleep#:~:text=A%20Lack%20of%20Sleep%20Affects,poor%20decisions%20and%20take%20risks [accessed 11/5/22].

27. Stephen R. Covey, *The 7 Habits of Highly Effective People'* (Fireside, Simon & Schuster, 1989), Pt 1.

28. Risa Williams, *The Ultimate Time Management Toolkit: 25 Productivity Tools for Adults with ADHD and Chronically Busy People* (Jessica Kingsley Publishers 2022), Ch 1., Pg 40.

29. 'Ways That Humor Can Heal' - https://psychcentral.com/health/ways-that-humor-heals#does-laughter-improve-health [accessed 4/8/22].

30. Churchill quote: https://youtu.be/gXR6DtJD8vg

31. John C. Maxwell, *The 15 Invaluable Laws of Growth* (Center Street, 2012), Ch. 11.

32. John C. Maxwell, *The 21 Irrefutable Laws of Leadership* (Harper Collins 2007), Ch. 18.

33. Risa Williams, *The Ultimate Time Management Toolkit: 25 Productivity Tools for Adults with ADHD and Chronically Busy People* (Jessica Kingsley Publishers 2022), Ch. 1, Pg 36.

34. Proverbs 13 v 20, *The Holy Bible,* New Living Translation, (Tyndale House Publishers Inc. 1996, 2004, 2015).

35. Trevor Stockwell (& other authors), *8 Qualities For Great Leadership* (Yeukai Publishing Services, 2023) Ch. 1.

36. John C. Maxwell, *The 21 Irrefutable Laws of Leadership* (Harper Collins 2007), Ch. 17.

37. Proverbs 27 v 17, New American Standard Bible, The Lockman Foundation. Copyright © 1960, 1971, 1977, 1995.

REFERENCES

38. Paul Scanlon, *Crossing Over* (Nelson Books, 2006), Ch. 12.

39. Variation of Proverbs, Ch. 20 v 5, *The Holy Bible.*

40. John 8 v 7, *The Holy Bible,* English Standard Version. ESV® Text Edition: 2016. Copyright © 2001 by Crossway Bibles, a publishing ministry of Good News Publishers.

About the Author

Trevor Stockwell is an independent Maxwell Leadership Certified Team member and DISC Trainer with 20+ years of leadership experience in the corporate and nonprofit sectors. He coaches and trains business leaders, entrepreneurs, and managers, empowering them to live more fulfilled lives. Trevor achieves this by raising their inner game, enhancing their self-leadership, and maximising their external results when leading others.

Mentored by John Maxwell, the world's #1 leadership expert, Trevor's passion for values-based leadership and empowering others to be more successful is the 'why' behind what he does. He is convinced that every individual has SO MUCH MORE potential than they realise or currently utilise, and often, external assistance is the catalyst for people to see and develop this.

He conducts one-to-one and group coaching and training. He is also the co-author of the Amazon #1 international bestseller, *8 Qualities For Great Leadership* and regularly gives back to the community by volunteering his time and skills.

"Our success is hidden in how well we lead ourselves."

Connect with Trevor and discover more
about

Trevor Stockwell Leadership Development Services

trevorstockwell.com

@tsleadershipdev

8 Qualities for Great Leadership
— critical elements for current and future success

The international #1 Amazon best-seller!

To become and continue to be an effective leader, there are critical key qualities you need to develop and demonstrate regularly. These qualities never expire and are universal, although they may be expressed in a myriad of ways depending on the circumstances, culture, and how you are wired as an individual.

Drawing on the insights, expertise, and leadership experience of eight authors, *8 Qualities for Great Leadership* provides practical information covering enduring leadership qualities essential for leading effectively today and future-proofing your leadership within an ever-changing marketplace.

Trevor's chapter, *'Self-Leadership: Raising Your Inner Game Maximises Your External Results',* focuses on three important self-leadership areas: Insight, Clarity, and Flexibility, which interact with each of the other elements.

The book also covers:

- Emotional Intelligence
- Intentional Leadership
- Leadership Resilience – Individual and Collective
- Leading Virtual/Remote Teams
- Improving Communication and Engagement
- Building Trust

- Designing Your Growth Strategy (B2B)

These qualities are not only essential for personal development but also for your team(s) and should be reviewed regularly.

More info here.

Printed in Great Britain
by Amazon